MW01414915

ChatGPT IS A MONEY-MAKING MACHINE

UNLOCKING THE POWER OF AI TO MONETIZE YOUR LIFE AND SECURE A LUCRATIVE FUTURE

Added Value:

- ✓ 7 Life-Altering Hacks
- ✓ Plugins/ Extensions
- ✓ Playground Feature
- ✓ Business Opportunities

Ideal for early AI adopters looking to monetize their interest

MICHAEL WOODS

Copyright © 2023 by Michael Woods. All rights reserved. No part of this book may be reproduced or transmitted in any form or by any means, electronic or mechanical, including photocopying, recording, or by any information storage and retrieval system, without permission in writing from the author. The information in this book is provided "as is" without warranty of any kind, either express or implied, including but not limited to the implied warranties of merchantability, fitness for a particular purpose, or non-infringement. The author and publisher are not liable for any damages whatsoever arising out of or in connection with the use or inability to use this book, including but not limited to direct, indirect, incidental, special, or consequential damages or loss of profits, even if advised of the possibility of such damages.

FREE GIFT JUST FOR YOU!

Our comprehensive career guide will help you find a fulfilling career path that aligns with your desired lifestyle. Discover a wealth of diverse job options, practical business startup advice, unique and exciting business ideas, as well as valuable college degrees that are worth the investment.

Download NOW for exclusive access to these insights.

Or go to http://michaelwoodslife.com/

TABLE OF CONTENTS

INTRODUCTION 1
CHAPTER 1: A Tour of AI Capabilities 3
    The AI Revolution: How is Changing Our World 3
    Who Can Benefit From ChatGPT: 6
    ChatGPT Capabilities and Uses: 9
CHAPTER 2: ChatGPT to Enhance Productivity and Income: .. 13
    Revolutionizing Entrepreneurship: A Game Changer: 16
    The Evolution of Entrepreneurship in the Coming Decades: 20
    How to Begin When You Don't Know Where to Start 24
    Business Examples of Rapid Scaling Through AI 27
    Identifying Profitable Online Business Opportunities: 36
    Freelancing in the AI Era: The Future of Work: 44
    There Is No Such Thing As Completely Passive Income: 51
    AI for Digital Products: 52
CHAPTER 3: Provoking Creativity: The Art of Prompts 61
    It is Just About Feeding it the Right Words: 61
    What is a Plugin? 64
    Prompt Precision: Unlocking Success with Clarity 67

Integrate Keywords Everywhere with ChatGPT 73

Hack # 1 Use The Playground Feature: 76

Hack #2: Have ChatGPT Create Prompts For You 79

ChatGPT for Content Creation: 81

Dealing with Lengthy and Complicated Prompts: 85

CHAPTER 4: Bring AI Into Everywhere You Work 88

AI in Daily Lives and Business: 88

Writing with AI: 91

You have to Fact-Check your Outputs: 101

Humanizing AI Generated Content: 102

Hack #3: Use The Browsing Beta In ChatGPT4: 107

Hack # 4 Get Advice In Your Particular Situation 109

Hack#5: Download the WebChatGPT Extension 115

CHAPTER 5: Learning Smarter 117

AI-Assisted Learning 117

Best Practices for Using ChatGPT for Learning: 121

Hack #6 Teach it to Write Like You and Create Content in Your Own Style 129

Hack #7 Summarize 131

AI, The Future of work and the Next Chapter of Human Progress 132

INTRODUCTION

Things are going to get very interesting, very fast. We are living in an era of fast technological change. Words like "Artificial Intelligence" or "AI" are no longer confined to the pages of science fiction novels or the labs of high-tech companies. AI is here, and it's here to stay. And while we're all aware of its growing importance, not everyone knows how to make the most out of it, especially when it comes to generating an income.

That's where this book comes in. My name is Michael Woods, I'm an Author and entrepreneur. I have grown multiple online businesses, and my goal is to help you understand ChatGPT, what it is, how it works, all you can do, and show you the ways it can open up a whole new world of opportunities for you.

I've designed this book with the "average Joe" in mind—just average people who simply wish to learn and want to make it happen. All you need is an open mind, a readiness to explore new opportunities, and the desire to turn AI's potential into your reality. AI might seem complicated, but it is not.

I want you to transform that spark of curiosity into a flame of opportunity. ChatGPT has the potential to revolutionize your productivity and income.

We won't stop at theories or concepts. Throughout this book, you'll find a wealth of business examples where ChatGPT can be used to scale rapidly. These examples will provide you with a clear blueprint for how you can leverage AI in your own ventures. If none of those businesses clicks with you, we'll also dive into the process of identifying business opportunities that align with your interests, personality, and current situation.

We understand that each person is unique, and there's no one-size-fits-all approach to success. That's why this book is designed to help you carve out your own path armed with the power of AI.

And not just that, we will cover plugins and extensions. Providing multiple recommendations for you. We are providing you 7 powerful hacks where you can use ChatGPT to improve your daily life. We will cover ChatGPT for writing and learning, we provide you with prompt examples to illustrate, and a lot more.

So more than just a guide, this book is a tool. A tool that can help you transform the potential of AI into tangible income and success. You'll discover an array of strategies tailored to your unique situation and aspirations.

So now you know that you don't need to be a tech expert, computer whiz or an experienced entrepreneur to reap the benefits. Immerse yourself in the content, read at your own speed, and practice as you learn. Remember, progress matters more than perfection. Happy learning!

CHAPTER 1

A TOUR OF AI CAPABILITIES

The AI Revolution: How is Changing Our World

The world will never be the same. As we step into the age of Artificial Intelligence (AI), it's becoming increasingly evident how this revolutionary technology is shaping our lives, regardless of whether we actively use it or not, understand it or not. An AI revolution is unfolding across various industries and fields. The world is set to undergo dramatic changes in the coming years, and by the end of this decade, our surroundings will be a lot different from what we're accustomed to today.

Driverless cars and virtual reality it is just the beginning, as time goes on many AI tools and applications will keep coming as different AI companies continue dropping their software to the masses to use, and every single aspects of our lives are going to dramatically change.

ChatGPT from OpenAI is a crucial player in this technological shift. It is the one who is starting all of it. This game-changing tool is transforming the way we communicate, access information, and interact with technology. In just a few months since its launch, it's already making a significant impact across different sectors, and it's superior natural language processing abilities have unlocked new possibilities for everyone. Not long after its debut, ChatGPT hit a major milestone by garnering 100 million monthly active users in just two months. This extraordinary growth pace has set a new record in user acquisition speed among consumer apps.

HOW LONG IT TOOK TOP APPS TO HIT 100M MONTHLY USERS

ChatGPT is estimated to have hit 100M users in January, 2 months after it's launch. Here's how long it took other top apps to reach that:

APP	MONTHS TO REACH 100M GLOBAL MAUS
CHATGPT	2
TIKTOK	9
INSTAGRAM	30
PINTEREST	41
SPOTIFY	55
TELEGRAM	61
UBER	70
GOOGLE TRANSLATE	78

SOURCE: UBS

yahoo/finance

ChatGPT is only the beginning. Many similar tools will keep coming in as AI will keep getting smarter and smarter. With not even a year of its release by mid-2023, it is already transforming content creation and disrupting many industries. Things like journalism, marketing, blogs, and anything related to content that you read online or offline is already being filled with AI. In one way, is it very good since this allows professionals to increase productivity, enhance their work, and it also brings many business opportunities for those early adopters who get early to make a ton of money.

ChatGPT is spearheading innovation and growth in today's digital world. The ways we work and earn are rapidly evolving. The operations of businesses have changed significantly compared to just a year ago. As you delve into this book, you will explore the extraordinary world of ChatGPT and uncover the boundless opportunities it offers. This journey will unveil how you can leverage this disruptive technology to fit your unique needs, accelerate your progress, and secure long-term personal benefits for yourself and those who you care about.

So we know you purchased this book because you want to learn how to use it to your personal benefit, and you do not want to be left behind in this revolution, you want to be one of the early adopters. Since ChatGPT and AI are bringing innovations in today's digital world by changing the way we work, learn and create, this has opened up many different opportunities for entrepreneurs freelancers, and aspiring income creators.

We want you to understand AI and ChatGPT and gain a solid foundation about all of the possibilities of this technology and its uses in various aspects of life specially when it comes to making an income and building wealth. We will explore many different AI tools, such as plugins and extensions where you can increase your productivity, expand your career possibilities and create new income streams. Whether you're an entrepreneur, freelancer, or looking for innovative business ventures, we'll provide practical insights and strategies to optimize your professional pursuits. You will also learn how to interact effectively with ChatGPT by crafting engaging prompts and integrating keywords to produce the desired output.

Numerous lucrative opportunities are emerging. You will find profitable business opportunities where you can use ChatGPT to scale quickly and ways to find businesses that will fit your persona. We'll provide a thorough exploration of how you can identify these opportunities and capitalize on them using AI. You'll gain insights into the sectors where AI can be a game-changer and learn how to use this knowledge to your advantage. Whether you're launching a new venture or looking to innovate within an existing business, the information in this book can guide you to make strategic and profitable decisions.

But AI isn't just for business, it can simplify almost every aspect of our daily lives. So the hacks you will find later in the book are designed to integrate it into your life to increase efficiency, simplify it and and make you more productive and efficient.

This book transcends the boundaries of being simply for AI aficionados or business experts. It serves as a universal compass, guiding all who wish to tread the path of progress. It is deliberately crafted to help you navigate the ever-evolving labyrinth of the digital universe. It arms you with the potent tools and indispensable knowledge to not just survive but to truly thrive both personally and professionally.

So, as we stand at the dawn of a new era, the question isn't whether you will participate in the AI revolution because you will be one way or another. The question is, how quickly can you adapt and thrive? How soon can you transform the challenges of today into opportunities for the future?

Who Can Benefit From ChatGPT:

ChatGPT has endless capabilities that you can use to your benefit. Regardless of where you are in life, you can mold it to the way you work. The versatility of this tool allows ordinary people to harness its capabilities in many aspects of llife and work. So no matter where you are, your profession, background, or interest, understanding ChatGPT can help you improve your life and help you get whatever it is you want out of life.

This book is designed for individuals of **all backgrounds:**

- Aspiring Income Generators
- 9-5 Employees
- Students
- Entrepreneur/Business Owner
- Freelancers
- Researchers
- Career Professionals

Everyone in this category can benefit from the teachings of this book.

Aspiring Income Generators:

If you are reading this book because you want to learn how to use it to make money, you are in the right place. This book will help you unlock the potential of ChatGPT and AI technology to create income streams. You are going to be introduced to the most typical online businesses out there and also ways to find opportunities. You will learn how to leverage this AI tool for things like content creation, marketing, leveraging business ventures, etc. You will discover innovative ways to monetize your skills and knowledge. The book will also provide strategies for identifying and capitalizing on emerging trends and already-established business opportunities within the AI-driven economy. So you will learn how to achieve financial stability and build a sustainable income in the age of AI. And it is still early, so get excited.

9-5 Employees:

People who still have jobs and are in the market can benefit significantly from using ChatGPT and its various applications. With the plugins and extensions you will be presented with, it can help you with work or outside of work, you can increase productivity and open up new ways of creativity by integrating this tool into your everyday routine. In less than 10 years, this will be the norm, but those who are still early will get amazing advantages. At the same time, the more you learn how to use it, the better ideas you will have to start something on your own. You will have increased career options, better work satisfaction, and improved job performance. You can be put in a better position to succeed in a job market that is evolving very fast.

Students:

If you are a student, either at school or college. This will massively benefit you. In later chapters, you will see unique tips that can enhance your educational experience. You will be learning how to use ChatGPT to assist with studying aspects such as homework research and learning. This will improve your understanding of topics and help you excel in your studies. Also, understanding this AI tool will give you a competitive edge in an increasing AI-driven job market. The more familiar you get with this technology, the better you will be for the economy that is coming. So as a student, learning to use ChatGPT will open doors, create new career paths and opportunities and prepare you well for the future of work.

Entrepreneurs/ Business Owners:

You can transform your business significantly if you learn how to use ChatGPT. It will no longer be an option but a necessity to learn about AI as an entrepreneur. You will learn to leverage tasks such as market research, content creation, customer support, and other related things to improve your business. Business owners can optimize their resources, refine processes, and drive growth. Adopting AI technologies for your business or ventures can help you stay competitive, enhance creativity and facilitate the creation of goods and services that address the needs of developing markets. If you understand ChatGPT, it can be a game changer for you as an entrepreneur or business owner. It will help you stay ahead of the curve and achieve long-term success in today's business world. You are not going to stay behind.

Freelancers:

Freelancers are probably the ones who are going to be using these technologies the most since they are always working with different types of online tasks. You will probably still get hired to do those pieces of work that businesses would still want to outsource, Think about it, they can do them themselves with AI, but many times they won't because they want to focus on other aspects of their business and they still want certain tasks to be outsourced. So Chatgpt can improve the effectiveness of your work and help you differentiate yourself for jobs like content writing, research, data analysis, marketing, and other related freelancing tasks. Since they can complete tasks much faster, freelancers may take on more assignments and ultimately earn more money by streamlining their processes and boosting productivity. Also, it can dramatically improve the quality of your work.

Researchers:

This will help researchers tremendously. ChatGPT has an enormous database, and it can enhance your potential to find out topics by learning to use ChatGPT for jobs like data gathering, reference finding, and getting insights into numerous issues. Researchers who read this book will be better prepared to use AI technology effectively and advance the frontiers of human knowledge.

Career Professionals:

As a professional, you want to stay up to date-and react rapidly to technological changes that will affect your sector. AI is expected to disturb many industries, and it will likely affect your industry as well. After all, AI will soon become more prevalent and a crucial talent to possess. So since AI has the potential to disrupt your industry you want to keep in touch with AI advancements, and Learn to use ChatGPT can help you enhance your performance in your profession with things like efficiency, productivity, research, and learning. Even if your job is not involved directly with AI, it can be beneficial for navigating the changing world marketplace.

ChatGPT Capabilities and uses:

The sky is the limit when it comes to using ChatGPT to venture onto the path pf progress. Think about ChatGPT as a tool to simplify your life, enhance your skills, expand your possibilities, become aware of the opportunities, and get you in the path of getting whatever it is you want out of life. And one of the most important things, make an income and create the lifestyle you want.

This is a unique opportunity that you have in your life; never in history has this happened where such a revolutionary technology was so in its early days, you were aware of it and you have access to it. You will never find yourself in a situation like this.

I am going to provide you with different things this amazing AI tool can do for you.

ChatGPT <u>Can:</u>

- Assist people in developing passive income streams.
- Help 9-5 employees improve their productivity.
- Assist individuals in coming up with profitable business ideas where you can use ChatGPT itself to simplify operations and accelerate the path to profitability.
- Assist entrepreneurs and business owners in generating innovative ideas and strategies for their businesses.
- Offer suggestions on how to monetize personal skills or expertise, such as creating an online course, starting a coaching service, or launching a blog.
- Support researchers in gathering and analyzing data, as well as generating insights from their findings.
- Assist career professionals in staying current with industry trends.
- Provide guidance for freelancers in optimizing their portfolios and attracting more clients.
- Offer students strategies for effective studying and help them balance their academic and personal lives.
- Guide individuals looking to improve their digital literacy by explaining concepts and suggesting learning resources.
- Assist individuals in formulating professional emails, letters, and other written correspondences.
- Suggest platforms and resources where one can learn skills that are in demand for remote or freelance work.
- Provide guidance on how to build and optimize a personal brand online to attract potential income opportunities.
- Help in creating a business plan or strategy for monetizing a hobby or personal interest.

- Provide an overview of how to make money online for those interested in starting an online business.
- Assist in evaluating the feasibility of business ideas.
- Assist in the creation of digital products or services, an area that many may not realize they have the capacity to explore. This could range from creating an eBook, developing a course, or offering consulting services in an area of expertise.

These are just a few of the many ways ChatGPT can be used to improve your life and income. This doesn't account for all the specialty tasks you can perform with plugins on specific business models. You can make operations more efficient and less complicated due to the nature of the business itself, such as in publishing, marketing, blog creation, and everything related to readable content.

So to conclude that ChatGPT can help everyone in their life whether is with work, business or profession. You don't know what you don't know It is up to you to use the information you get from this book and apply it to your specific circumstances in life.

Keep in mind that in life to get what you want, you need to know how. Our knowledge guides us and the type of access we have to it is broken down in three parts.

Known Knowns: These are things that we are aware of and understand. For example, if you're an accountant, you know how to file taxes - it's a known known. You know what it is and you have a fair amout of knowledge about the topic.

Known Unknowns: These are things that we are aware they exist of but do we not understand. We know what they are but we have gaps in knowledge that haven't been filled yet. For example, you may know Crypto and its existence but you may not know how it works.

Unknown Unknowns: These are the things we don't even know we don't know. So we are not aware of them and indeed do not understand. These are gaps in our knowledge that we aren't even aware exist. It's somewhat harder to give a concrete example here, because by definition, these are things we're completely unaware of.

These limitations might be your current state of AI technology itself, in your case most likely the second option: you know it's there and you know you can use it to your personal benefit but you don't understand of how to effectively utilize it to take advantage of it like so many people are.

CHAPTER 2

CHATGPT TO ENHANCE PRODUCTIVITY AND INCOME:

There is an abundance of opportunity for wealth creation. The AI revolution is still in its infancy and it has already created a few millionaires already, for the most part are people who were already growing a business, recognized the opportunities and applied it. They were able to enhance and speed up their growth. Many AI operations are vast and largely unexplored. For example, AI's role in big data analytics is expanding, and its ability to extract meaningful insights from massive amounts of data could provide businesses with a competitive edge, leading to increased profitability.

ChatGPT can help you identify profitable business opportunities and make the operation of the business easier, It can help you predict future trends, recognize market patterns, and suggest ideas for businesses that are most likely to be successful and you probably would have not think of if it wasn't for AI. All of this makes it so much easier than ever before to start a business. So use the information you are getting to make informed decisions and seize lucrative opportunities.

To successfully leverage the power of AI to create a sustainable income requires a strategic approach. You need to know the steps involved to start from someone who doesn't know anything about AI and is lost about the many different businesses to start to someone who has an idea of the process of which someone who knows nothing can make an income.

So here are 6 key steps that pave the way for leveraging ChatGPT and turning it into a valuable **income-generating tool:**

Step 1: Get to know ChatGPT, how it works and unleash it's potential.

Keep reading this book and learning about how ChatGPT works. The more you understand about it the more effectively you can utilize it. Use the teachings while getting hands-on yourself with the tool. Dive deep into it's abilities, boundaries and familiarize yourself with various applications, plugins, and extensions available to enhance your interactions with the tool. There's no better way to learn than by doing.

Step 2: Identify A Business Opportunity:

If you do not know what type of side project or business to start yet, no worries we have all been there at some point, the good news for you is that you have the most useful tool to figure it out. You need to start leveraging AI capabilities to analyze market needs gaps and different types of businesses. We have a full section about this shortly where we are going to be introducing you with the most typical and well-known online business out there and also going to teach you how to find many other business opportunities that are perfectly customizable to who you are, what you know and the situation you're in.

Step 3: Use ChatGPT to enhance your skills in the relevant area.

Once you have identified a business opportunity, it's time to leverage the potential of ChatGPT to enhance your knowledge and skillset in the relevant area. Natural language processing and machine learning can be used to build extremely accurate conversations that will assist you in comprehending how your industry or business functions. You can use it to understand and become aware of ways to escalate and find potential solutions to your industry-specific problems. You will learn how to ask questions, explore ideas, and even simulate scenarios that would specifically apply to your business and get the answers you need.

Step 4: Identify Your Unique Product or Services:

There is going to be competition in whatever business or industry you will get in, competition will always be there. To stand out you want to clearly articulate what are you going to offer. You need to understand your target audience and define the specific product or services you are going to provide. You can use AI to brainstorm potential product or service ideas based on your understanding of the market needs. All of this will help you start preparing and visualizing your startup journey.

Step 5: Start and learn along the way.

Imperfect action is better than perfect inaction. You do not need to have all the answers and be an expert to get started. By simply taking action and getting started you will get your feet wet and gain valuable learning opportunities that will refine your approach along your journey. You need to embrace a mindset of continuous learning and improvements as you navigate the challenges and complexities of your entrepreneurial journey.

You will keep learning as you go and do, you need to get started to get feedback. Do not attempt to have all the answers before you have the questions. learning on the way also enables you to seize opportunities that may arise unexpectedly. With an open mind and a willingness to adapt, you can capitalize faster.

Success | **Success**

what people think it looks like | *what it really looks like*

Keep this in mind. The path of success is rarely linear. You are going to encounter uncertainties and challenges, and that's ok, that's how its supposed to be. When it comes to business the best way to not fail is with innovation and adaptation in your field. You always have to be improving in adapting to circumstances, and when it comes to AI is no different. As AI continues to evolve, your business will continue to evolve. So the potential for growth and income is limitless. AI can be used to create a world of possibilities for yourself, and ChatGPT is leading the way into this revolution, and this is just the beginning, more similar AI tools will continue to come.

You just need to fall in love with the process adjust your approach when necessary, keep learning things related to your industry, and focus more on progress than perfection. If you apply these things, you'll be building a thriving AI-powered business using ChatGPT in no time.

Revolutionizing Entrepreneurship: A Game Changer:

When it comes to entrepreneurs and "wantrepreneurs"— meaning individuals who want to start their own businesses—it is essential to learn about AI. The world is changing, and adaptation is critical and if you are stock in the old ways you are not going to get too far. If you don't adapt, you risk being left behind and missing out on significant potential revenue. If you take the time to learn and adapt, you can maintain profitability and stability for your company or venture. Here are different aspects of your business where ChatGPT can provide assistance:

- Marketing
- Copywriting
- Greater business knowledge
- Website creation
- Market research
- Trend analysis
- Competitor analysis
- Product development
- Customer feedback analysis
- Branding and positioning
- Social media strategy
- Content creation
- Customer service improvement
- Email marketing
- Search engine optimization (SEO)
- Sales funnel optimization

You probably felt a little overwhelmed with the amount of help you have from AI to take your business to the next level and that is a good thing because you realized that AI can help you in pretty much every aspect of your business or venture.

Entrepreneurs always struggle with numerous challenges when it comes to finding innovative solutions and capitalizing on market opportunities. Running a business was never easy, actually is quite hard. But with the advance of AI technologies, these obstacles have just become a lot easier to overcome than ever before.

Typical challenges are now easier to overcome with ChatGPT:

As we mentioned before, embarking on an entrepreneurial journey is never easy. You will find obstacles on the way; expect that things will come up, and you have to deal with them when they come and as they come. The good news is that now you have ChatGP, which is your resourceful assistant available around the cock to help you navigate thru these challenges. This will transform the landscape of entrepreneurship forever.

I am going to provide you with different hypothetical scenarios of typical entrepreneur challenges and how with the help of AI, you can overcome them:

Scenario 1: Wantrepreneur Seeking Scalable Business Idea

Imagine you are a 'wantrepreneur' (Meaning you want to become a business owner) eager to venture into entrepreneurship. You are tech-savvy and have a strong desire to leverage AI, specifically ChatGPT, to start a business that could scale rapidly. However, you're unsure about the kind of business you want to start and the steps needed to bring this vision to fruition.

- Strategy: Use ChatGPT to guide you through idea generation, validation, market research, and initial business planning. Given its vast knowledge base, ChatGPT can provide insights into potential markets and business ideas that can leverage AI for scalability.
- Prompt Example: *"ChatGPT, I'm interested in starting a business that can easily scale with the help of AI. Could you provide suggestions on potential business sectors and specific ideas that would benefit from AI integration?"*

Based on the information you feed into ChatGPT, the AI can suggest various ideas that align with current trends and market gaps. For instance, it might suggest starting an AI-powered personal finance app, an online learning platform, or a chatbot service for businesses, amongst other things, once there you can keep following up to gain more insights and personalized things for your own special circumstance.

Next, you could ask ChatGPT for the steps to take after choosing a business idea.

Prompt Example: `"I have decided to start an AI-powered personal finance app. Can you guide me through the next steps I need to take to establish this business?"`

ChatGPT could then provide you with a roadmap detailing necessary steps such as market research, competitor analysis, business plan creation, product development, branding, marketing strategies, and many more.

Again, remember that while ChatGPT can provide valuable insights and recommendations, the final decisions will depend on your judgment, your risk tolerance, and your personal passion and commitment to the business idea.

Scenario 2: Crafting a Unique Value Proposition

A tech entrepreneur is struggling to articulate a unique value proposition for her new mobile app that aids in mental health management.

- Strategy: Use ChatGPT to brainstorm the unique features and benefits of her app and how these can translate into a compelling value proposition.
- Prompt Example: `"I need help crafting a unique value proposition for my mental health management app, which uses AI for personalized recommendations and community support features."`

In this example you are requesting directly the help you need

Scenario 3: Competitor Analysis

A new restaurant owner is in a competitive neighborhood and he needs to understand his competitors better in order to carve out his own niche.

- Strategy: Use ChatGPT to analyze the strengths and weaknesses of competitors based on the available data for his specific restaurant, location and specific competitors.
- Prompt Example: `"Here's a list of five competitor restaurants in my area, along with some recent reviews and their menus. What strengths and weaknesses can we identify from this data and how can I overpower them?"`

Our exploration of hypothetical scenarios demonstrated how this AI could be utilized strategically to navigate typical entrepreneurial challenges. If you are lost in a sea of business expansion possibilities or a wantrepreneur seeking a scalable business idea, ChatGPT can act as your compass, helping you chart a course through these complexities. It is critical that you know that you need to keep your human judgment or "gut" when it comes to knowing which route you should take. You must be the decisive element and use your intuition, risk tolerance and passions to keep your business into the right path.

The Evolution of Entrepreneurship in the Coming Decades:

At this point you know that entrepreneurship is going to evolve and it will dramatically change, since AI will make it easier for people to persue ideas and faster to capitalize on those ideas. We are going to be breaking down different aspects of this revolution in simple sections

The Democratization of Entrepreneurship through AI:

With AI the barriers and obstacles that many people had from pursuing entrepreneurship are shrinking. A democratization process in underway and to make it incredibly accessible to everyone. Entrepreneurship will be easier for most people to start, so there will be an increase in the number of entrepreneurs.

This impact can be attributed to two key factors: First, AI tools like ChatGPT simplifies and automates complicated tasks, which allows business owners to focus on other aspects of their business and also, people aspiring to own a business feel more attracted to the idea to start. There will be more time for entrepreneurs to dedicate to creativity, innovation, and strategic planning, the cornerstones of a successful business.

Secondly, AI simplifies other aspects like data analysis, web development, and marketing. All without the need for extensive expertise and training. The emergence of AI has given rise to a new breed of entrepreneurs who can leverage these tools to turn their innovative ideas into thriving businesses. So we can expect to see an increase in the number of entrepreneurs worldwide. This is because AI tools lower the barriers to entry in many ways.

The Shift in Business Models:

We are going to see an increase in shifts in business models. The infusion of AI technologies into various sectors is enabling businesses to break free of human limitations, expanding the realm of possibilities for entrepreneurial ventures. Traditionally, many business models were constrained by human limitations, such as the inability to process vast amounts of data quickly or to work around the clock. Now with AI that is changing, machine learning automation among other things, is overcoming these limitations, which were unattainable under traditional models. As we look forward into the future of entrepreneurship, we can envision several types of new business models emerging, largely enabled by advancements in AI and technology, such as personalized services, predictive businesses, on-demand services, and mass customization, among others. The future of business will look different as technology and society continues to evolve.

The Evolution of Decision Making: Data-Driven Insights through AI

Entrepreneurs always had to be a critical part of the decision making of a business and this shapes the course of direction for that business. Traditionally, these decisions relied on past experiences and intuition, and sometimes even guesswork. Not with AI machine learning technologies, this may be transitioning into an era of data-driven decision-making, since AI can automate en enhance decision-making processes by analyzing vast amounts of data and providing actionable insights. This is very transformative especially for entrepreneurs who very often face uncertainty in business and have a hard time thinking a path forward.

Take the example of understanding customer behavior, traditionally understanding their preferences and predicting future trends required a fair amount of conjecture. Now AI can analyze large datasets of customer interactions, purchasing history, and social media activity providing amazing-useful insights and data information to make decisions in product development, pricing strategies, marketing campaigns, and more.

All of this predictive analysis can assist entrepreneurs with decision making. It can identify emerging market trends, potential risks, and opportunities, allowing entrepreneurs/ business owners to strategically position their businesses for future growth and success.

So all of this is good. AI and machine learning are fundamentally changing the way entrepreneurs make decisions and operate their busines. So we can say we can expect faster growth. There will be less guesswork and intuition and more data-driven decision making. Overall This would not replace human decision-makers but provide accurate insights, leading to better-informed decisions. This comes to the conclusion that in this evolving landscape, embracing AI is no longer optional for entrepreneurs but a critical enabler of their success.

The Long-term Vision:

We can be certain that AI will continue to shape entrepreneurship. It will continue to take on roles there were once exclusive to humans, and more and more it will change the paradigms of what it means to be an entrepreneur. Future entrepreneurs might need to possess a solid understanding of AI principles and ethics and be adept at working closely with AI, much like a skilled artisan with their tools. Everything will change; almost every related work will require some sort of AI tool, and new business models will emerge. This AI-driven evolution will not be confined to a single geography or industry; the trend of globalization will continue to connect business owners from all corners of the globe, enabling the sharing of innovative ideas and practices in AI utilization. Moreover, the role of education will inevitably transform to meet these new demands, offering courses and programs that focus on the intersection of AI and entrepreneurship, equipping the entrepreneurs of tomorrow with the skills they need to thrive. So with all of this is safe to say the many less business will fail.

If you have more questions about how entrepreneurship will be affected, I will leave you 10 different questions/prompts you can ask ChatGPT:

1. "How will AI technologies shape the landscape of entrepreneurship in the coming future?"
2. "What changes can we expect in the dynamics of entrepreneurship due to advancements in AI?"
3. "Can you provide examples of new types of businesses that are likely to emerge as a result of AI advancements?"

4. "What skills and knowledge will be crucial for entrepreneurs in an AI-dominated business landscape?"
5. "What are some potential challenges entrepreneurs might face as they increasingly rely on AI in their businesses?"
6. "How might AI technologies democratize entrepreneurship, making it accessible to a broader range of people?"
7. "In what ways might AI alter the business models we see today? Can you provide a few hypothetical examples?"
8. "How could AI impact decision-making processes in entrepreneurship?"
9. "What role will AI play in the scalability of future businesses?"
10. "What are some ethical considerations for entrepreneurs incorporating AI?"

How to Begin When You Don't Know Where to Start

If you don't know where to start when it comes to using AI to generate an income for yourself, it is totally ok keep reading this book, and you will be on your path to progress. Forward in the book, we are going to be providing different business examples for you where you can use ChatGPT to scale quickly, if none of those examples work for you, you will see a section that helps you find different businesses that will match your current situation, personality, and circumstances.

Keep something in mind: There is a time for action, and there is a time for research. Meaning that when you are unsure of where to start, you need to give yourself a certain period of time to figure it out, which is what you are doing right now by reading this book.. Also, focus on progress more than perfection, perfection is unrealistic in most cases. No one is perfect, and no task is ever done perfectly. It's about learning, improving, progressing and accepting that failure is part of the process.

Continue Learning

You want to keep learning about ChatGPT, AI, and different businesses and ways to monetize. While at the same time, practice and use ChatGPT to be more familiar with the tool and brainstorm ideas yourself. Monetizing AI takes several forms. I will provide you with many of these forms for you to choose what you want to pursue and go with it.

The more you use ChatGPT, the more familiar you are going to be with it while, at the same time, you will realize its potential while you learn about different business models and ways to monetize it. If you want to make money online, you should have basic comprehension skills about how the world works and how making money online works. ChatGPT serves as a powerful tool to enhance and speed up the process, but you will need foundational knowledge. The more you learn, the better equipped you are to take action. Yet, each action you take, each experiment you conduct, is in itself a form of research - a learning experience that adds to your understanding and proficiency. You also need to work on your patience because it is true that you can use AI to move quicker with different business models, but at the same time, having the knowledge in your head to do this effectively will take time.

Different ways to monetize ChatGPT/AI:

Early adopters of new technologies, including AI, often reap significant benefits. Catching trends early, always leaves you in a much better position than doing them later. And the good news for you is that even if you are reading this in 2025, you are still early when it comes to AI because it keep evolving for decades to come.

Here are some ways that people are monetizing AI:

Starting a Business where given its nature, you can use ChatGP scale quickly:

There are a lot of different businesses out there (We are providing examples shortly) where given the nature of the business, you can use AI to scale it and grow much faster than not having AI—for example, Social media marketing, Eccomerce, KDP publishing ETC. There are a lot of different industries where this can apply. It can help on most ventures that you want to get yourself in, you want to choose certain businesses where growing it typically would take five years, with the help of ChatGPT would take 2. This gives you a significant competitive edge and allows you to stay ahead of the curve.

Develop AI Skills and Offer Freelance Services: By mastering ChatGPT, individuals can offer their skills as consultants or freelancers. I am not expanding more here because we have a whole section on freelancing later in the book.

Investing in AI Companies: A more long-term approach, but as well one of the most direct ways to monetize AI. There is no secret that some massive companies will exist in the future that provides AI services that today are small to medium size companies. You can invest in public AI companies or private startups. Investing in a small to medium-sized company that grows considerably over 10+ years can be a very rewarding experience, both financially and personally.

Apply it to your current venture or profession: If you already have a venture, business or profession that you are doing, there is likely an aspect that you can use to help you scale quickly, maybe you can apply it with marketing or better product descriptions or better customer service or decision making, AI can be a powerful tool in enhancing various aspects of your current venture or profession, and it can be the ultimate tool to take it to the next level.

Business Examples of Rapid Scaling Through AI

In the following section, we will dive into various business examples where you can harness the power of ChatGPT to scale quickly. Many of these businesses are still prevalent today and will most likely be around for years to come. There are so many, and you will probably see models that you never heard before. I want to let you know that I will be providing a quick overview of the business and how you can use ChatGPT to scale quickly. Since I will be providing an extensive list and each of these businesses could easily merit a book of its own, you will need to do further research about the business model if it interests you. This is supposed to make you aware of what's out there in the online business world and encourage you to use the following sections as starting points in your exploration of these exciting opportunities.

E-commerce: It is basically commerce but online that's where the E comes from, "Electronic" " refers to the buying and selling of goods or services using the internet.

You sell goods or services online directly to consumers. It Can be general or niche-specific.

There are different types of Ecommerce.

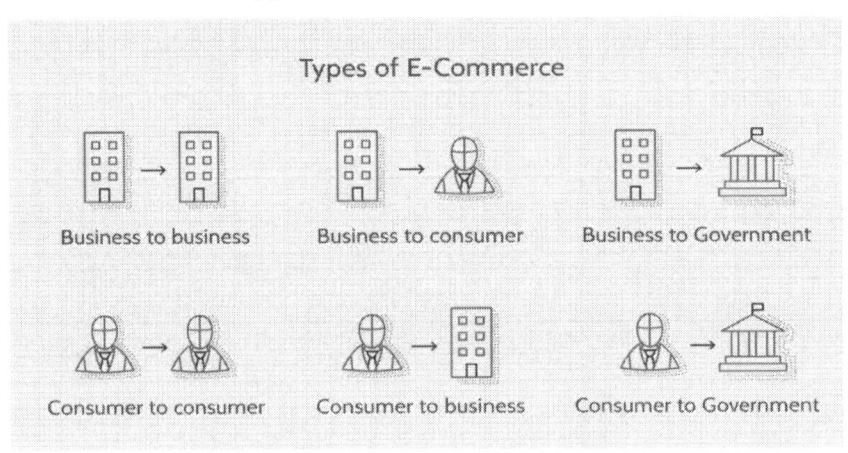

Types of E-Commerce

- Business to business
- Business to consumer
- Business to Government
- Consumer to consumer
- Consumer to business
- Consumer to Government

There are numerous hosting platforms that you can use for your e-commerce business, like Shopify, WooCommerce or Bigcommerce.

And as As for what you can sell, the possibilities are virtually endless. It can be Physical goods, digital products (We will cover this in a later chapter), or services.

- Where ChatGPT can enhance and speed up the growth:
- Providing personalized product recommendations.
- Writing engaging and SEO-friendly product descriptions.
- Website content
- Generating creative ideas for marketing campaigns.
- Assisting in creating engaging content for social media promotion.
- Coming up with ideas of what products or services to create.
- Helping you learn and understand eccomerce.

Social Media Marketing Agency (SMMA): You help businesses with social media strategies, content creation, ad management, and other related services to enhance their online presence and help them grow their business for a monthly or yearly fee. They basically pay you to help them grow and get customers by providing marketing services and social media management services.

- Where ChatGPT can enhance and speed up the growth:
- Prospecting: ChatGPT can help automate the process of finding and identifying potential clients.
- Creating personalized proposal drafts for potential clients
- Marketing Campaigns: ChatGPT can assist in creating compelling narratives and unique selling propositions for marketing campaigns,
- Website Content: ChatGPT can help generate engaging and SEO-optimized content for the website of these clients.
- Ad Copy: ChatGPT can aid in writing persuasive ad copy for various platforms such as Google, Facebook, Instagram, and more. The marketing you run for these clients of crucial for their success
- Helping you understand your customer's business and provide ideas of actions to take to help them grow.

- Social Media Posting: Within seconds, you can generate content to cover extensive periods for your agency's own social media platforms, thereby maintaining a consistent online presence
- Report Generation: ChatGPT can help automate the generation of internal reports, such as sales performance or client engagement metrics, aiding decision-making and strategy planning.
- Email Marketing: Generating emails either for yourself of your clients
- By feeding it the right data, you could use ChatGPT to draft preliminary reports on the performance of different marketing campaigns,

Youtube Automation: I am going to give you a more extensive description of this business model because it is truly great. In this business model, you can create videos from already existing content on the internet. Pick a niche, add a voice, and compile them in different ways to make a video. You can post about one video per week and grow the Youtube channel where you mainly pick up youtube advertising. You can mainly outsource a video editor and voice actor to make the videos for you or you can make them yourself if you have little money. The goal is to generate enough ad revenue to cover all expenses and leave a profit for the channel owner each month. It is very cheap to start and easy to scale.

It doesn't take that much to get started. Creating a video will take (Completely outsroucing everything) From $100-$300 per video. If you pick a good niche (specific consumer group/ Segment of the market), if you create high-quality videos, and you post 3-4 per month, you could see yourself making thousands of dollars per month in less than a year.

- Where ChatGPT can enhance and speed up the growth:
- Brainstorming Ideas: Use ChatGPT to generate a wide range of ideas for your YouTube content. You can provide the AI

with a general theme or topic and ask it to generate unique and innovative content ideas.
- Script Writing: Use ChatGPT to create scripts for your YouTube videos for your editor. You can provide the AI with the main points or structure of the video, and it can generate a detailed script.
- YouTube Description: ChatGPT can help in creating engaging and SEO-friendly descriptions for YouTube videos. This can help in improving the visibility of your videos on the platform.
- Channel Strategy and Planning: Use ChatGPT to develop a comprehensive strategy for your YouTube channel, including content planning, audience targeting, and growth strategies.
- Audience Analysis: ChatGPT can help in analyzing your target audience and providing insights on their preferences and behaviors. This can help in creating content that resonates with your audience1.
- SEO Optimization: This means generating SEO-friendly titles and tags for the videos. Which is essential to making your videos attractive to viewers.

Amazon FBA (Fulfillment by Amazon): With this business model you are basically selling physical products on Amazon. You ship your product to Amazon's warehouses, and Amazon handles storage, packaging, and shipping to customers who buy your product. So you provide the overhead of physical products, and they are sold on the Amazon platform. This business model typically requires a high investment of more than $5000 USD, but it can be very profitable if you do it well.

- Where ChatGPT can enhance and speed up the growth:
- Assisting in writing engaging product descriptions.
- Generating ideas for products in high demand and low competition

- Generating creative ideas for Amazon-specific marketing campaigns.
- Assisting in managing inventory
- Providing insights for improving Amazon product listings based on customer interactions.

Sales Funnel Creation: This business model is when you have something to sell, whether a digital or a physical product, you build a series of steps designed to guide visitors toward a buying decision, often through landing pages using softwares like Clickfunnels, email marketing, and other strategies, while you also typically build a brand around it as well. It is a great way to sell a valuable product to the masses. It is a way of Eccomerce as well.

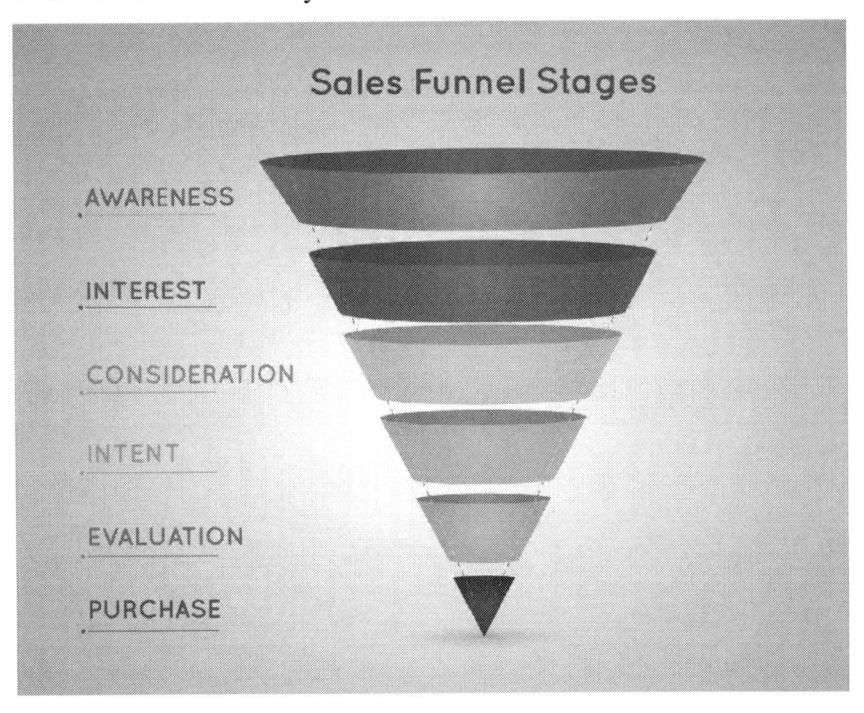

Sales Funnel Stages

- AWARENESS
- INTEREST
- CONSIDERATION
- INTENT
- EVALUATION
- PURCHASE

So you have a whole process constructed that people will go thru, you move down the funnel from awareness to purchase, and the number of people at each stage generally decreases. This is a natural part of the process of a funnel, as not everyone who becomes aware of your business and your product will be interested, not everyone who's interested will consider purchasing, and so on. But that is not a reason for concern. A well-constructed sales funnel will ensure that a high proportion of those who enter the funnel eventually make a purchase. The better the funnel, the higher percentage at the bottom will be. This can be very profitable if you have a good product to sell. As for what to sell, just like we mentioned earlier it can be anything of value to a section of the market.

- Where ChatGPT can enhance and speed up the growth:
- Coming up with ideas of what products or services to sell in the funnel
- Creating persuasive copy for landing pages, emails, and other elements the funnel.
- Generating creative ideas for improving sales funnel strategies.
- Assisting in creating the content for the whole funner process (Each stage and the emails as well)
- Help you with the marketing copy

Basically, ChatGPT can help you with all the content creation for the funnel, the good thing about this business model is that if you have a good product, you put the work out front to sell it, and if the funnel is good, you can just leave it, and it could sell for years.

Dropshipping Business: This is another form of Eccomerce. You have an online store, and you sell products to the public, these stores can be easily built with websites like Shopify or WoCommerce. But you don't keep products in stock. Instead, you purchase the item from a third-party website and have it shipped directly to the customer while you keep the difference. Kinda like Retail arbitrage; you buy low and sell high, the beauty of dropshipping is that you only buy the product once the product has already been purchased from you, So there is no overhead or inventory risk. Most of these products are outsourced from websites like Alibaba or Aliexpress. Some people have deals with different suppliers where they get a discounted price.

The Dropshipping Process

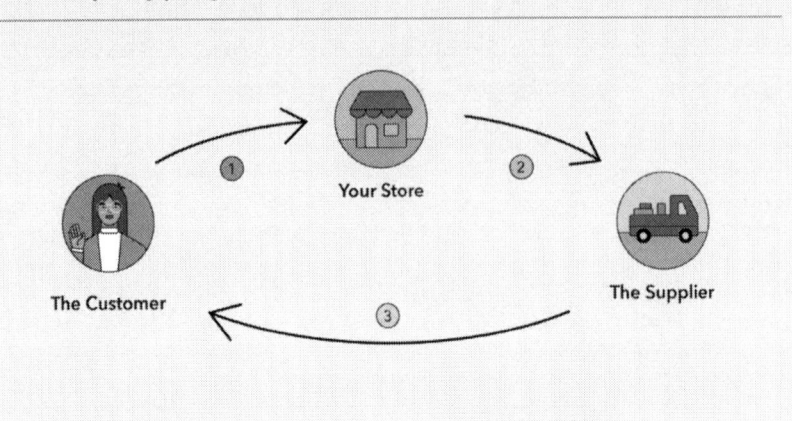

- Where ChatGPT can enhance and speed up the growth:
- All the content for your dropshipping website. (Product description, home page, checkout,etc)
- Crafting good emails to suppliers to let you drop-ship their products
- Content for all of the marketing campaigns
- Email sequence content to customers
- Automating responses to customer reviews and feedback.
- Generating ideas for marketing dropshipping products.
- Assisting in creating engaging content for social media promotion.

Digital Marketing Agency: Very similar to SMMA but more focused on marketing. You offer different types of online marketing services for businesses, including SEO, Social Media, content marketing, email marketing, and more. You can use ChatGPT for all of the content creation and ad copy since ChatGPT is great at copywriting. With this, typically, you had to outsource it and pay money, now, you can use ChatGPT to do all of this much faster. So if you have marketing skills and can consider freelancing with ChatGPT.

Affiliate Marketing: Promoting other companies' products and earning a commission for each sale made through your referral link. Every time people click that link and buy the product, you get a commission of the sale. Many websites that you are familiar with, like Bestbuy, Walmart, Amazon, etc, offer affiliate programs. You have to find people who are already looking for these products online and market it to them with your link. When they purchase from you, there is nothing that you need to do, just get the sales commission. You only have to make sure that people who are interested in buying something from Bestbuy for example click your link and there are many techniques and ways to do this. There are already a segment of the market that are purchasing things and you only have to make sure that they use your link when they do so.

The more you sell with that link the more commissions you will have.

Where ChatGPT can enhance and speed up the growth:

- Writing persuasive product reviews or descriptions that encourage readers to click on affiliate links.
- Generating creative ideas for promoting affiliate products.
- Helping you understand how to market these links
- Getting ideas for websites offering affiliate programs and markets where you can cap into.
- Assisting in creating engaging content for affiliate marketing promotion.

Web Design and Development Services: You only create new websites for businesses or individuals or improve existing ones. If you have skills in website development, this can be a great task that you can freelance. You can charge hundreds, if not thousands of dollars for a website.

- Where ChatGPT can enhance and speed up the growth:
- Create high-quality written content for the whole website
- Create email project proposals for clients

- Generating creative ideas for improving web design strategies.

Ebook Writing and Publishing (KDP): Just like this book that you are reading right now, you can create and sell digital books online on various platforms like Amazon KDP and audible. You cannot write a whole book with AI since Amazon has AI content detectors, and they will remove your book. But you can come up with basically content ideas and help you compile the information necessary for the book. You can also hire a ghostwriter to write it for you.

- Where ChatGPT can enhance and speed up the growth:
- Assisting in the writing process, providing suggestions for plot development, character creation, and more.
- Help you with book descriptions, copyright pages, and other nonbook-related content.
- Writing engaging marketing copy.
- Generating creative ideas for book promotion.
- Help you with Amazon A+ content.
- Providing insights for improving book writing and publishing based on reader interactions.

Virtual Assistant Services: Providing administrative, technical, or creative assistance to clients remotely, you can offer your services on different websites online like Upwork, Fiverr, Freelancer, and Zirtual, among others.

There are a lot more different types of businesses, and we cannot name them all, these are just to give you an idea of what's prevalent in the market today and what you can do depending on your abilities. The possibilities in the online business landscape are virtually limitless. The above examples are by no means exhaustive, and there are many other business models out there, each with its own unique nuances and requirements, and many of them where you can use ChatGPT to scale much faster.

The key to identifying a business that is correct for you in your current situation is to assess your skills and passions, understand the market dynamics, identify the demand, know your target audience, and then tailor your offerings accordingly. If none of these businesses sound appealing to you, the following sections will help you in how to find a profitable business that matches what you want.

Identifying Profitable Online Business Opportunities:

It has become easier than ever to analyze and identify potentially profitable business opportunities. If you know how to, ChatGPT can help you spot these within seconds; this will allow you to make quicker decisions about investments and help you locate your time and resources more efficiently.

You may be in a position right now where you don't know what business to start, you may be aware that there are multiple businesses out there that you can do, and AI tools like ChatGPT can help you enhance many of those business models and help you scale much faster than it would typically take. You may have a business already and you are looking for golden nuggets to be able to scale it a lot faster. Whatever it is we will have information about this for you

In order to be able to identify these business opportunities, you want to have at least an idea about your current market and digital trends, and how the world of online business works. Of course, ChatGPT can help you with this by providing you with valuable insights into customer behavior, what products and services are in demand, and which niches have potential growth. It can also help you identify untapped markets with similar products and services that have yet to be explored. The more you understand about your potential venture, the better business launch you will have, do not forget to assess your own skills, passion, and resources to align with profitable business models that will work for you in your current situation.

Keep this in mind. There is no necessity to reinvent the wheel, there are a lot of established businesses, such as E-commerce and digital consulting, just to give you a few examples, these continue to thrive and most likely are not going anywhere any time soon. Instead of coming up with a new idea, focus on finding a businesses that already exist and do your best to implement it better. Provide a better value proposition, superior, product and with a fresh marketing strategy, you can distinguish yourself from the competition and your business can thrive. You don't need to be the first at something to succeed. By getting into a proven business model you can mitigate some of the risk of starting a new venture. By doing all of this, you will have a unique approach to stand out in a crowded marketplace.

Uncovering potential online business ventures: key factors to consider and prompt examples to help with your research:

"Can you explain the different types of online businesses and how to choose the one that suits my skills and interests?"

"I enjoy technology and creativity, what kind of online businesses could potentially align with these interests?"

"Can you tell me about the current market trends and opportunities for starting a new business?"

"What are the steps to validate a business idea and ensure there is a market demand for it?"

"I'm passionate about fitness and health, what type of business opportunities exist in this field?"

"I want to start an online business but I'm on a tight budget, what are some low-cost startup ideas?"

"Can you provide a list of skills that are in high demand for online businesses? I want to consider upskilling in these areas."

"I want to start a business that makes a positive impact on society. Can you provide examples of social entrepreneurship?"

"Can you explain how to leverage AI tools like yourself to streamline a business that I can scale quickly?"

"I want to start a business, but I'm worried about the time commitment. How can I manage my time effectively as a new entrepreneur?"

These prompts should help provide direction and guidance to those who are unsure about what type of business they should start. They can help uncover your passions, align them with your skills, and match them to a business model that has potential in the current market.

A question that you may be asking yourself is how can an aspiring entrepreneur take advantage of AI to fill gaps in the market and create a business that can scale quickly. You first must understand the potential of this technology, how to use abilities, and remember that AI can exceed human capabilities in many respects, once you have this knowledge, it will be easier for you to observe industries, analyze market gaps and capitalize from your data analyses. Entrepreneurs who can bridge these gaps with AI will pave the way for scalable businesses that could dominate their respective markets. AI technology will continue to advance, and the possibilities for entrepreneurial innovation are vast, promising an exciting future for scalable, AI-driven businesses.

How to evaluate the business once you have chosen it:

1. **Market Trends:** Observe current and emerging trends in your industry and the broader market to spot potential opportunities.

Prompt Examples:

- "What are the current trends in the eCommerce industry?"
- "Can you outline the emerging trends in online publishing?"
- "What are the recent developments in SEO marketing?"
- "What changes are currently happening in the digital marketing sector?"
- "Could you explain the latest trends in affiliate marketing?"

2. **Target Audience:** Know your ideal customer well to identify gaps in the market that your business could fill.

Prompt examples:

- "Can you describe the typical consumer for an online fitness platform?"
- "What are the characteristics of the target audience for eco-friendly e-commerce stores?"
- "What are the needs and preferences of customers using online travel agencies?"
- "Who is the primary audience for home automation systems sold online?"
- "Can you profile the typical buyer of eBooks?"

3. **Skills and Passion:** Align your skills, interests, and passions to find the right business opportunity for you.

Prompt Examples:

- "I have skills in graphic design and I love animals. What online business opportunities might align with this?"
- "What kind of online businesses can I start if I'm passionate about sustainable living and have experience in e-commerce?"
- "What digital industries could benefit from my background in software development and my interest in healthcare?"
- "I have a background in finance and love to cook. What are some online business ideas that might be suitable for me?"
- "What opportunities are there in the online entertainment industry for someone who's passionate about film and has experience in digital marketing?"

4. **Competition:** Analyze the competitive landscape to determine how your business can stand out.

Prompt Examples:

- "Who are the main competitors in the online vegan skincare market?"
- "Can you list the top five companies in the digital learning industry and

describe their unique selling propositions?"
- "Who are the key players in the digital renewable energy sector, and what sets them apart?"
- "What is the competitive landscape in the online fitness industry?"
- "Could you outline the competitive dynamics in the direct-to-consumer e-commerce fashion industry?"

5. **Profitability Potential:** Evaluate the potential profitability of the opportunity to decide whether it is worthwhile.

Prompt Examples:

- "What is the potential profitability of starting an online coffee supply business?"
- "Can you describe the financial viability of an online mobile application development company?"
- "What is the potential return on investment for an online solar energy information platform?"
- "What are the revenue streams and potential profitability for a digital subscription box service?"
- "Could you provide a profitability analysis for an online boutique hotel booking platform?"

6. **Resource Availability:** Assess what resources you have or can acquire to make the venture a success.

Prompt Examples:

- "What are the necessary resources for starting an online software as a service (SaaS) company?"
- "What equipment and resources do I need to start an online craft tutorial platform?"
- "Can you list the human, material, and financial resources required for launching an e-commerce platform?"
- "What resources are needed to open an online yoga instruction platform?"
- "What are the assets and resources required to start a virtual reality gaming company?"

7. **Scalability:** Consider the potential for growth now and in the future to ensure long-term profits.

Prompt Examples:

- "What is the scalability potential of an online cloud kitchen business?"
- "How scalable is an online digital marketing agency?"
- "Can you explain the scalability considerations for an online software development startup?"
- "What factors should I consider when assessing the scalability of an online tutoring service?"
- "How can I evaluate the scalability of a 3D printing service?"

8. **Risk Evaluation:** Identify and mitigate financial, operational, and market-related risks.

Prompt Examples:

- "What are the major risks associated with starting an online AI technology company?"
- "Can you list the potential financial, operational, and market-related risks of opening an online restaurant?"
- "What could be the potential risks for a company in the online esports industry?"
- "What are the key risks associated with an online fintech startup?"
- "Could you help me identify the potential pitfalls of an online green energy consulting service?"

9. **Sustainability:** Consider the long-term sustainability of the venture, including environmental and market sustainability.

Prompt Examples:

- "ChatGPT, can you outline some considerations for making an online fashion brand more sustainable?"
- "What are the key elements to consider in order to make an online food delivery business environmentally friendly?"
- "How can an online tech company ensure long-term sustainability in terms of both market trends and environmental impact?"

- "What are some best practices for making a digital logistics company more sustainable?"
- "Can you explain how an online coffee supplier can implement sustainable practices in its operations?"

It is now simpler than ever for you to understand what you are getting yourself into before diving into it. ChatGPT will help you analyze patterns in market data and unlock insights that you will need to know before making your next business move. Making quick decisions can result in issues that can easily be avoided. This will also help you stay ahead of the competition by providing market intelligence about products, services, target audience preferences, pricing strategies, and more.

It is ok to dive into it and experiment especially when you are young, you will still make mistakes, but the best prepared that you are, the better. Entrepreneurial accomplishments aren't overnight; they're actually quite slow and require meticulous growth over time and you have to stay committed to providing value to what you are doing. Therefore, take some time to think, analyze, and plan before you start an online or offline business. Be willing to try new things, but keep in mind that any worthwhile endeavor need regular work and development. Fall in love with the process.

Freelancing in the AI Era: The Future of Work:

Before getting started let me tell you what freelancing is: Freelancing is a form of self-employment where you offer your services to clients on a project-by-project basis, without a long-term employment or contract. Even though AI is revolutionizing the way most tasks can be done, not everyone will take the time to learn everything and do it themselves, so freelancers will still be needed for years to come. There is still a need for human skills, creativity, and expertise. AI enhances human capabilities but they don't replace the need for interpersonal skills that humanize the work being done.

No one feels comfortable consuming something they think was all written by a machine when a person is behind it.

Here are a few reasons why freelancing will remain valuable:

- Unique Creativity: AI can generate content based on patterns and rules but can't truly replicate human creativity and innovation. AI falls short in having the content it creates connect with individuals on a human level, is not quite there yet, maybe it will be at some future. For roles like writing long formats of text like books, personalized design, and other creative fields, human freelancers are still irreplaceable, businesses will probably still hire people for this, so AI is not just there yet to replace humans.
- Specialized Knowledge: To be able to be a freelancer in a specific niche you need a deep understanding of complex subjects and being able to communicate with the business owner on a human level, something that AI is not capable of fully doing (YET). AI won't change that businesses want to outsource different aspects of their business.
- Interpersonal Skills: This is basically human communication. tasks that require empathy, deep understanding, and effective communication with clients are best done by humans. This includes roles like coaching, counseling, and consulting, something that it could by replaced by AI if it gets to crazy levels, but it will take a little while.
- AI Understanding and Management: This may sound ironic but the rise of AI creates its own demand. There's a need for professionals who understand AI technologies and are able to implement, manage, and troubleshoot these systems. People will still be needed to manage AI.
- Customization: It is true that AI can automate many tasks but it often falls short when customizing something in a certain way or when unique solutions are required. Humanf

freelancers can offer personalized services tailored to each client's needs, with the help of AI of course.

After knowing that AI will not fully replace freelancing, you should be exited to get starting knowing it will make your work 100 times easier and faster than ever. The most valuable asset for independent contractors/freelancers is their talents and expertise which they use to benefit their clients.

Now being a successful freelancer requires more than just having a certain set of talents; it also requires the ability to effectively advertise those skills, manage projects, and build trusting relationships with clients. You are not just selling a service, you are selling a solution to their problems, a quality product or service, and a positive experience.

Here are some of the most common gigs in the freelance world:

- **Writing and Editing:** If you are a person that's good at writing, this freelance gig could be the perfect fit. With the help of AI this is a lot easier, it allows you to create content for blogs, ghostwriting for professionals, write copy for advertisements, etc. Now having said all of this, AI will definitely disrupt this industry. The impact of AI on the demand for writers is complex, in the short term, we may see a decrease in demand for certain types of writing work but it is hard to predict how it will evolve in the long run.
- **Graphic Design:** Businesses are always on the lookout for talented designers to create logos, websites, and marketing materials. If you have an eye for design, there are plenty of opportunities for freelance work. (This one can be replaced by AI soon but you can probably still use it for clients who don't want to use AI for themselves)
- **Web Development:** Website creation was always in high demand.

- **Social Media Management:** This is considered a type of freelancing, if it grows big it turns into a more than just a gig: A profitable business
- **Consulting:** Same as social media management, in the beginning stages, it is considered to be a freelancing gig
- **Virtual Assistance:** Organizational and administrative skills are valuable to businesses as a virtual assistant. They manage different tasks like emails, schedules, data entry, and more.
- **Translation:** If you're fluent in multiple languages, translation services are in high demand for businesses with global reach. Although it is hard to predict how AI will affect this industry, most likely it will replace humans translators very soon.
- **Photography or Video Editing:** Digital media skills, including photography and video editing, are sought-after for businesses looking to elevate their online presence.
- **Tutoring or Teaching:** If you have a talent for teaching, online tutoring services are a great option for education-focused freelancing.
- **SEO Expertise:** Businesses need help with search engine optimization to improve their visibility online. If you're savvy with SEO, you could offer your services as an independent contractor.
- **Narration and Voiceover Work:** If you have a clear, articulate voice and excellent reading skills, narration and voiceover services are a great way to put your talents to use. Disrupting in this industry with AI will probably be very high
- **Copywriting:** Copywriting is the art of selling with the written word. Persuasive writing is highly valued in advertising and marketing. With tools like ChatGPT, you can offer even more value to clients by generating ideas and drafts. Disrupting here will be high.

- **Editing:** If you love diving into language and grammar, editing services may be for you. Freelance editors can proofread documents, refine written content, and improve the structure and flow of writing. ChatGPT is perfect for this.
- **Project Management:** Coordinating projects and leading teams is a valuable skill in many industries. As a freelance project manager, you can help companies navigate complex projects and campaigns.
- **Data Analysis:** Businesses need data analysts to help them make strategic decisions. If you have a head for numbers and an eye for detail, you could provide data analysis services as a freelancer.

Writing about how freelancing can help with any of these gigs will take a full book on itself, I am giving you these gigs for you to know what are the most common freelancing gigs and how ChatGPT can enhance your capabilities and become a powerful ally in your journey. Use it to generate ideas, draft proposals, or even automate routine tasks, AI can help you offer better services, free up time and automate different types of work. You can also use it to brainstorm content ideas.

Upwork and Fiver are the most popular online platforms where freelancers can market their skills and connect with potential clients. Both of these digital marketplaces serve a wide range of businesses and industries and present different opportunities for independent contractors to showcase their expertise.

Upwork and Fiver are the most popular websites/platforms where freelancers can market their skills, offer their services and connect with potential clients. These online markets serve a wide range of businesses and have unique feauures for freelancers to market themselves.

Both websites are similar. When it comes to upwork, you can promote yourself with businesses of all types all around the world, connect and work together on projects. Typically you will find professionals that are a little more expensive on Upwork than on

Fiverr. You can create a profile about your past experience, past employment, hourly rates, and availability. In order to demonstrate their qualifications to potential clients, they might also offer their work history and portfolio. On Upwork, freelancers can search for and apply for jobs that match their tastes and skill set. Businesses also have the option to invite you to specific job posts that they have for their business.

Fiverr on the other hand works a little different, freelancers are more to be picked for customers that are looking for gigs more than competing with other freelancers for tasks that those clients have listed. Potential clients tend to contact you to ask you questions about a gig they have, and you can negotiate what you will charge to the client., you can also offer different types of services on packages that clients can choose from. Projects there are typically inexpensive and short term compared to Upwork.

So both platforms are similar but at the same time work a little different. If you are thinking in providing services for clients, you can try both and see which one works better for you.

To simplify the steps you need to take from not being a freelancer to becoming a one, observe the following guidelines:

Self-Assessment: Start by evaluating your skills, expertise, and interests. Identify what kind of services you can offer that align with these skills and that are in demand in the freelance marketplace.

Market Research: Research your potential competitors. Check how they present their services, what rates they are charging, and what their clients say about them. This will help you understand how to position yourself in the market.

Create a Portfolio: Gather or create examples of your work that you can show to potential clients. If you don't have any work examples, consider doing some pro-bono work or creating mock projects to showcase your abilities.

Create Profiles on Freelance Websites: Set up profiles on websites such as Upwork, Fiverr, Freelancer, and Guru. These platforms can connect you with clients from all over the world. Make sure to create a compelling profile that highlights your skills, experience, and the services you offer.

Promote Yourself: Besides these platforms, promote yourself through social media channels like LinkedIn, Twitter, or Facebook. Also, consider creating a personal website or blog where you can showcase your portfolio, share your thoughts and ideas, and make it easier for clients to find and contact you.

Start Bidding or Applying for Jobs: Start bidding on projects that match your skills on the freelance platforms. Make sure your proposals are customized to each job post and clearly articulate how you can provide value to the client.

Deliver Quality Work: Once you start getting jobs, focus on delivering high-quality work and exceeding client expectations. This will help you build a good reputation and attract more clients.

Build Long-Term Relationships: Aim to build long-term relationships with your clients. Repeat clients can provide a steady stream of work and may refer you to other potential clients.

Use AI Tools: As you scale, consider using AI tools to streamline your business operations. For instance, AI chatbots can handle client inquiries, AI-driven project management tools can optimize your workflow, and AI-powered accounting software can automate your invoicing and financial management.

Keep Learning and Improving: Keep abreast of trends and advancements in your field. Continually upgrading your skills and adapting to the changing needs of the freelance marketplace will help you stay competitive and allow your freelance business to thrive.

You can be very successful if you are able to adapt, see the long-term benefits of freelancing and using AI tools like ChatGPT to scale your business. You have to be patient, persevere and keep refining your approach based on experiences and feedback from clients. Providing quality work and assist them in the best ways you can and fulfill that need, If you can solve a problem, fulfill a need or deliver a benefit with a skill you may have, then there is a market for it. The beauty of this is that it allows you to capitalize on something that you know which also may be your passion and you can turn it into a professional endeavor. So, consider what you're good at, what you enjoy doing, and how you can provide value to others. Freelancing typically starts small but it can turn into big things.

There Is No Such Thing As Completely Passive Income:

I am sure you have heard about the term passive income multiple times. The term may not mean what I am about to tell you, but implies that you can earn money with little to no effort consistently for years. Many online gurus have widely popularized this concept promising a life of leisure and freedom while the money keeps rolling it. Don't get me wrong, you can get very close to something like that but it is mostly the exception rather than the rule. There is no such thing as COMPLETELY passive income. Even the most passive-seeming income streams require significant effort, at least initially, to maintain.

You may be wondering, What about rental properties, what about a Youtube channel or investments? Managing rental properties include constant work remodeling, managing tenants, etc. A Youtube channel requires constant content creation, promotion, audience development, and engagement to continue to bringing revenue. And investments require careful preparations, a lot of study, and constant attention to financial markets to maintain your assets. So almost nothing is completely hands-off. All these income streams involve risks that must be actively managed. Rental properties can go vacant, investments can go down, and blogs or YouTube channels can see fluctuating views and ad revenue. I am not saying you should not pursue business ventures like these, but do not believe that you do not have to work to maintain a flow of money coming in. In reality, maintaining passive income streams is like maintaining a well-oiled machine. Consistent attention and care are required to ensure they continue running smoothly. Most businesses or income sources, even those dubbed as "passive," need ongoing maintenance to thrive.

Having said all of this, automation and outsourcing are ways to get closer to the idea of completely passive income, The more tasks you are able to outsource, the more hands-off you can be with your business. For example, property management companies can handle the day-to-day operations of rental properties, and virtual assistants or content creation teams can help manage a blog or YouTube channel. Financial advisors can manage investment portfolios. However, even with outsourcing, there's a need for active involvement. You still need to manage the team, make strategic decisions, and deal with unexpected issues.

Keep in mind that outsourcing and automating services are not free, so it costs money to buy your time back, and typically even if you have the money and you do end up, outsourcing all of this, it is probably to go work on something else rather than doing nothing. So there is always work that you are going to be doing. But the beauty is that you can enjoy what you do. So to summarize, the idea of passive income is feasible, you can get very close to it, and it can offer greater freedom and flexibility than a typical career or job, but it requires constant maintenance and effort.

AI for Digital Products:

A digital product is any product that's stored, delivered, and used in an electronic format. These products are intangible and are often distributed globally via the internet, making them accessible to anyone with a connected device. ChatGPT can be used to quickly and efficiently create digital products such as e-books, online courses, and software among others. This and other AI tools makes it easier for you to generate content that is engaging, relevant, and tailored for a specific audience. Also, the use of AI helps speed up the process of creating this allowing you to finish with your digital product a lot faster than you normally would. You can also use for feedback t and refine the product or service that you are offering.

So creating digital products with AI requires less manual labor than traditional methods, saving you time and money. So you can create a high-quality product without the need to invest vast resources in personnel.

Here are some examples of digital products:

- Online Courses and Webinars: Online courses where people just buy them once and watch them, only courses are becoming a lot popular and they are not going anywhere anytime soon.
- Ebooks and Digital Books: These can be non-fiction (how-to guides, informational books, etc.), just like the one you are reading right now. They can also be interactive ebooks or PDF guides where you can sell on Amazon in the Kindle Direct program.
- Software and Apps: If you have programming skills, you can create software, mobile apps, or web apps. Typically creating these types of products requiere a high investment.
- Stock Photos and Graphics: If you're good with photography or graphic design, you can create and sell your own stock photos, illustrations, icons, templates, or fonts. There are a lot of websites where these are being offered such as iStock, Shutterstock, and Element, among others. Although it is likely that AI will disrupt this industry significantly
- Music and Sound Effects: Musicians can sell their own music tracks, sound effects, or even customized jingles.
- Online Consultation or Coaching: If you're an expert in a particular field, you can offer one-on-one consulting or coaching services on video directly to people, it is not a digital product itself but you are offering your expertise yourself online.

- Membership Sites: These are sites where people pay a recurring fee to access exclusive content or services. Some examples of this includes educational platforms, Fitness programs or even entertainment like Netflix or HBO Max. Online courses can also fit into this category.
- Digital Art and Prints: Artists can sell their work as digital downloads. These can include digital paintings, printable art, or 3D models. (Likely to be disrupted)
- Online Tools or Services: Any online tools you use, this might include SEO services, social media management tools, budgeting tools, or other online tools that help people solve a problem. They will become more popular as time goes on,

How ChatGPT can help with content creation and marketing of digital products:

Creating Digital Products:

- Content Generation
- Curriculum Development
- Design Assistance (Different AI tools)
- User Experience Improvement

Marketing Digital Products:

- Target Audience Research
- Messaging and Copywriting
- SEO Optimization
- Social Media Promotion
- Email Marketing
- Pricing and Monetization Strategies
- Customer Support
- Analytics and Insights

There is a variety of reasons why digital products have a lot of advantages to business owners. They eliminate the need to physical inventory, so there is no concern about storing or shipping actual items, this makes administrative expenditures much lower. The challenges that usually come with conventional business models are minimized. This creates the possibility for a smaller, more flexible business operation where resources and time can be used for improving the quality of your product and marketing as well.

Also if you product is really good you can reach global audiences, also there is more room for errors because you can modify digital products quickly, this will make you stay on top of changing trends because you can always customize it and change things when needed.

It is a win-win for the creator and the customer. Here are some of the **benefits of digital products** for both.

For the Creator:

- No inventory management: This is a great plus, digital products eliminate the need to maintain physical stock, there is no need to keep inventory at your home or at a garage, this reduces costs and eliminates the risk of overstocking or understocking.
- No shipping requirements: Digital products are delivered electronically when someone buys them from you, you typically have a system set up where they recieve it automatically, there is no need for physical storage space or shipping logistics, this saves a lot of time and money
- Higher profit margins: Digital products typically have higher profit margins compared to physical products. This is becasuse of the lower production and distribution costs. For example with Amazon FBA you profit margins are shrink because of the cost of stocking and shipping.
- Passive income potential: Once a digital product is created and set up, it can generate passive income as it can be sold repeatedly without the need for continuous effort or active

involvement. Of course, you need to keep the marketing going and the brand alive, but besides maintaining that and the quality of the specific digital product there is not much else that you need to do for it to keep selling.
- Data-driven insights: Digital products provide opportunities to gather valuable customer data and analytics, allowing creators to gain insights into customer behavior, preferences, and purchasing patterns to inform business decisions and future product development.
- Flexibility and versatility: Digital products offer the flexibility to experiment with different product offerings, pricing models, and marketing strategies, enabling the creator to adapt and evolve their business based on market feedback and trends.
- Scalability: Digital products can be easily replicated and distributed to a large number of customers without additional production costs, allowing for unlimited scalability.
- Lower production costs: Once a digital product is created, it can be reproduced at minimal cost, resulting in higher profit margins compared to physical products.
- Rapid modification and updates: Digital products can be quickly modified or updated to incorporate new features, improvements, or market trends, enabling the creator to stay ahead of competitors and meet evolving customer demands.
- Automated sales and delivery: Digital products can be sold and delivered automatically through online platforms or websites, reducing the need for manual intervention and increasing efficiency.
- Global reach: Digital products can be accessed and purchased by customers worldwide, providing a global market opportunity and expanding the potential customer base.
- Diverse monetization options: Digital products offer various monetization models such as one-time purchases, subscriptions, licensing, or affiliate programs, providing flexibility to choose the most suitable revenue streams.

Benefits for the customers:

- Immediate delivery: When a cutomer buys a digital products they can be downloaded or accessed instantly after purchase, this allows customers to start using the product immediately without any delays. They dont have to wait for shipping unlike when they buy a physical product
- Convenience and accessibility: Customers can access digital products from anywhere, at any time, using their preferred devices, providing convenience and flexibility.
- Lower cost: Digital products often have lower price points compared to physical products due to reduced production and distribution costs, making them more affordable for customers.
- lifetime access: In many cases, customers receive lifetime access to digital products, allowing them to use and benefit from the product indefinitely without additional charges.
- Customization and personalization: Digital products can often be tailored to meet individual customer preferences or needs, providing a more personalized and tailored experience.
- Regular updates and support: Creators of digital products often provide regular updates, bug fixes, and customer support, ensuring that customers receive ongoing value and assistance.
- Environmental friendliness: Digital products have a minimal environmental impact since they do not require physical production, packaging, or shipping, making them a greener choice for eco-conscious customers.
- Access to expertise and knowledge: Digital products often provide access to specialized knowledge, expert advice, or educational resources that can help customers enhance their skills, gain new insights, or solve specific problems.
- Convenience of remote learning: Digital educational products, courses, or tutorials enable customers to learn from

the comfort of their own homes or wherever they prefer, eliminating the need for physical attendance or travel.
- Flexible learning pace: Digital educational products allow customers to learn at their own pace, enabling them to pause, rewind, or revisit content as needed, ensuring a personalized and adaptable learning experience.

Digital products have high benefits for entrepreneurs, and they are easier to create than ever. They are also quite new and still evolving, they will become more and more common with time. We are still undergoing a digital transformation, so the importance and relevance of digital products are growing exponentially. You probably have used one yourself already without noticing it. We can anticipate a continued shift towards digital products as consumer preferences evolve and technology advances. As a result, the ability to create, market, and distribute digital products effectively will likely become an even more critical skill for entrepreneurs and businesses.

Here are some prompts that can guide you in asking ChatGPT about the identification, market trends, profitability, and creation of digital products:

Identification:

- "How can I identify potential digital product opportunities?"
- "What factors should I consider when identifying a digital product opportunity?"
- "How can I identify a niche for my digital product?"

Market Trends

- "What are the current market trends for digital products?"
- "What is the future outlook of the digital product market?"
- "How does the current economic situation affect digital product trends?"

Profitability

- "What makes a digital product profitable?"
- "How can I determine the profitability of a digital product?"
- "What are the key metrics to consider when assessing digital product profitability?"

Creation

- "What are the steps to create a digital product?"
- "How can I make a digital product that stands out?"
- "What resources are needed to create a digital product?"

Miscellaneous

- "What are the challenges of creating and marketing a digital product?"
- "How can I market a digital product effectively?"

- "What are the top-selling digital products in 2023 and will likely remain relevant going into 2030?"

The goal here is to give you ideas and the knowledge you need to find the types of businesses that can fit your skill, interest and current situation. Each person's entrepreneurial journey is unique and driven by a different set of circumstances, so it would be an oversimplification to be suggesting one type of business. What we aim to do instead is to equip you with the right tools and understanding to leverage your unique strengths and navigate your unique challenges. ChatGPT can be used for exploration and discovery and provide you with many insights into various industries and strategies that would be blended with your personal knowledge, interests and unique situation. Entrepreneurship is very individualistic, and the foundation of it by learning how to use this AI tool we hope that you use this information to empower your discovery and create a business that is successful and uniquely suited to you.

CHAPTER 3

PROVOKING CREATIVITY: THE ART OF PROMPTS

It is just about feeding it the right words:

A prompt is basically the input that you write to ChatGPT OR whatever AI tool you may use to generate a response, it also be called a "query". This can be a question, a statement, a single word, or whatever you type for the language model or (Chatbot) to initiate a conversation or request a specific response. It is the initial input that you type to get the output.

When it comes to prompts, the quality of the user's input has a direct impact of the quality of the output, meaning the response you will get. A well-written and understandable prompt will result in more accurate and relevant responses than a prompt that was written poorly.

When you write a prompt that is poor quality, not very clear and with a lot of grammatical errors the response you will get from the system will be less satisfactory. It can also provide inaccurate or irrelevant information.

For example, using the prompt: *"What are your thoughts on the topic?"*

This prompt is vague and lacks the necessary details to generate a good response, it doesn't specify the particular topic you want to discuss leaving it open-ended and unclear.

A better prompt for something like that would be: *"What are your thoughts on the impact of Artifical Inteligence on job markets?"*

This prompt is more specific and provides a clear context about the topic you wish to discuss (Artificial intelligence) and the aspects you are interested in (It's impact on job markets). With that you give the AI system a clear direction on what you need, and you will get a more relevant response.

A few tips to keep in mind:

- The AI responds based on the date it was trained. You will notice it can sometimes be biased in supporting a specific movement. It gives great answers most of the time, but it has a hard time grasping common sense.
- You should evaluate your outputs and use your own reasoning when using the information given, especially if you are going to be using this for a school essay or putting the content on the internet you need to fact-check it and rephrase it.
- The way you phrase your prompt matters. By asking the question in a slightly different way, you can get a different response.

Here are more prompt examples that are well crafted:

"What are the main benefits of regular exercise for overall health and well-being?"

This simple and easy-to-understand prompt seeks an explanation of the main benefits of regular exercise for overall health and well-being. You are stating the topic of interest (benefits of exercise), and you are providing a clear direction on what to generate the content for.

"Could you please provide an analysis of the impact of renewable energy on global carbon emissions reduction?"

Another well-crafted and detailed prompt. It provides clear instructions and specific details about the desired analysis (impact of renewable energy on..). By providing this level of clarity and detail you are guiding ChatGPT to generate a response that addresses the specific analysis you requested.

"What are the key benefits of practicing mindfulness meditation for mental well-being?"

This simple and easy-to-understand prompt seeks an explanation of the key benefits of practicing mindfulness meditation for mental well-being. You are focusing on a specific topic and aspect of interest.

You can probably get a general overview of a topic by asking broad questions like *"Can you tell me about climate change?"*. However, if your prompts are more specific like *"What is the impact of climate change on ice caps?"*, the model's response will be more focused and tailored to that specific aspect of climate change.

The choice of words can also affect the tone and style of the response. For example, if you ask, *"What's the deal with quantum physics?"*, you may receive a more casual and informal response about the topic as the model will mimic the informal tone of your prompt. However, if you ask *"Could you please explain the principles of quantum physics?"*, the response is likely to be more formal and academic in nature.

What is a plugin?

When it comes to ChatGPT a plugin is a piece of software (The plugin itself) that adds specific features or functionalities to a larger application (ChatGPT)

Plugins are tools developed by third-party developers that allow ChatGPT to interact with their APIs, therefore enabling new use cases. What these plugins will do will depend of what the plugin is made for. These plugins are designed to extend ChatGPT capabilities and adapt it to the unique requirements of different applications It's essentially a way to connect ChatGPT to external, third-party applications, enhancing the AI's capabilities.

Subscription and Access: You must be a ChatGPT Plus subscriber to access plugins.

After enabling the plugins feature in your ChatGPT settings, you can install a plugin from the Plugin Store within ChatGPT

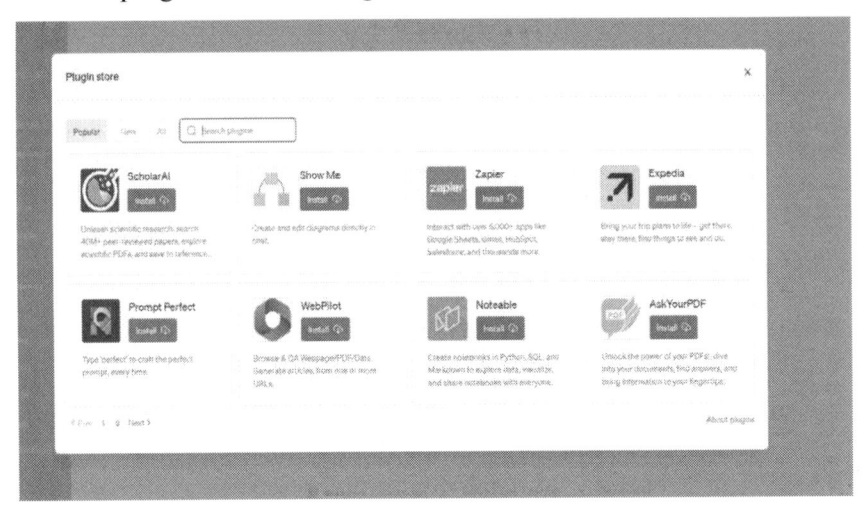

Over here, you can download the plugins, some are free some you may have to pay. You can select the plugin and start a conversation with a comand to use it.

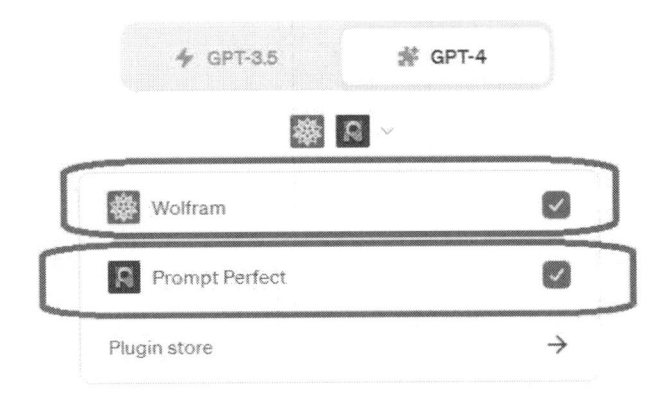

We will be providing different plugin recommendations for you to know what they are, and how different they are:

Wolfram:

The Wolfram Plugin for ChatGPT provides access to computational power, accurate mathematics, curated knowledge, real-time data, and visualization capacities of Wolfram|Alpha and the Wolfram Language. The 3 are products of Wolfram.

The plugin is as of now free. Once the Wolfram Plugin is enabled in a new chat session, it allows ChatGPT to perform a variety of enhanced functions using the power of Wolfram to give much better up to date and difficult responses.

In summary, the Wolfram Plugin for enhances the capabilities of the AI model by linking it with the computational and knowledge resources of Wolfram|Alpha and the Wolfram Language. To learn more about what you can do you can do a deeper reaserch of Wolfram.

Couper: Do you want to find coupons for everything?

The Couper plugin for ChatGPT is an extension that allows users to access coupon codes and cash-back offers directly within the ChatGPT interface. Allowing it to access up-to-date information, run computations, or use third-party services.

It is very easy to use, just ask the Chatbot to find you coupons for the specific things you want:

```
Please find me coupons for
```

```
I need discount coupons for
Provide coupons for
```

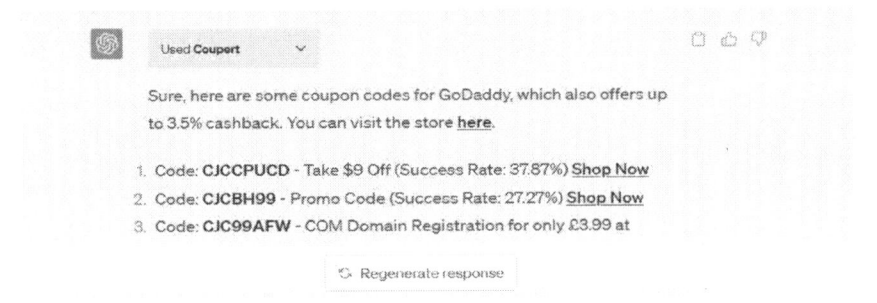

> Used Coupert
>
> Sure, here are some coupon codes for GoDaddy, which also offers up to 3.5% cashback. You can visit the store here.
>
> 1. Code: **CJCCPUCD** - Take $9 Off (Success Rate: 37.87%) Shop Now
> 2. Code: **CJCBH99** - Promo Code (Success Rate: 27.27%) Shop Now
> 3. Code: **CJC99AFW** - COM Domain Registration for only £3.99 at
>
> Regenerate response

After your request, if available, The plugin will help ChatGPT provide you with the codes, the details of the benefits of the code, and the link where you can take advantage of it.

They are well over 100 plugins out there that you can choose from. Find one that will enhance your productivity.

You can combine Plugins as well:

It is possible to combine different plugins in ChatGPT and use them simultaneously to get even better responses. The use of multiple plugins simultaneously can make your interaction with ChatGPT more dynamic and productive, as it allows the model to perform a wider range of tasks and provide more comprehensive responses. Sometimes plugins don't work and fail, and that's ok, it happens. Typically if you give it a second or third attempt, it will work just fine.

Prompt Precision: Unlocking Success with Clarity

Prompts are made up of 3 essential parts:

An Action - This is an active verb that initiates a response from ChatGPT.

A Structure - This refers to a specific structure that ChatGPT is instructed to follow.

A Direction - Any supplementary details that can enhance the quality and specificity of the output.

```
"Summarize the key points of the American
Revolutionary War in bullet points, similar to
a school textbook."
```

Action: `"Summarize the key points"`

This phrase directs the AI on what you want it to do – in this case, to summarize.

Structure: `"of the American Revolutionary War in bullet points"`

This part provides a clear structure for the AI to follow. It specifies the topic (the American Revolutionary War) and the format of the response (bullet points).

Direction: `"similar to a school textbook."`

This part gives additional guidance to the AI. It instructs the model to present the information in a way that's appropriate for a school textbook, which generally means clear, concise, and straightforward language.

Specificity is king. Imagine ordering meals at a restaurant and asking the server: *"Bring me some food"*. The server will be like, "Ok, well what type of food?" and he won't know what to bring you. Then instead of that imagine that you requested, *"Bring me the chef's special medium-rare steak with garlic mashed potatoes on the side."* This time, the server will know what to bring to you. It works similarly with AI tools like ChatGPT.

Keep in mind that being specific doesn't always mean you have to make the promps longer. It just means more precise. Sometimes a short specific prompt can be more effective than a longer prompt, for example:

```
"Can you tell me about some different types of
animals around the world and what they eat?"
```
This prompt is quite broad. It asks about animals all around the

world, which includes thousands of species, and their diets. This could generate a very diverse and possibly overwhelming response.

Shorter, more specific prompt: *"What's the diet of a panda bear?"*

This prompt is shorter, but it's much more specific. It asks directly about the diet of one particular animal, the panda bear. This would yield a concise and focused answer, which might be more useful if you're specifically interested in panda bears.

So being more specific—and not necessarily longer—can make a prompt more effective.

Having said that, long prompt have their place. A longer prompt can be useful when you are seeking a detailed and complex response from AI. For example, if you are asking for an analysis of a complex concept and you want to point out different things outlining different facts you want to use a longer prompt.

Longer, specific prompt: *"Please describe the process of making a chocolate cake from scratch. Include steps for preparing the batter, baking it, and making and applying frosting. Also, discuss how to store the leftover cake properly."*

In this prompt you are asking to provide a detailed response, It's not just asking for a general process of making a cake, it's specifying a chocolate cake and includes several distinct steps: preparing the batter, baking it, making and applying frosting. This type of detailed, specific prompt helps guide the AI to provide a comprehensive response that covers all the aspects you're interested in. In this case, it's not just about making the cake but also about what to do with it afterward.

The most common elements that make a prompt effective:

Command: This is essentially the action you want the AI to perform. It could be 'describe', 'explain', 'write', 'compare', 'contrast', 'summarize', and so on. The command sets the type of response you're expecting.

Example: `"Summarize the plot of 'To Kill a Mockingbird'."` (The command here is **"summarize"**, asking the AI to condense the plot of the novel.)

Subject: This specifies the topic you want the AI to focus on. It could be a person, a concept, an event, a place, a phenomenon, a literary work, etc. Basically just the topic at hand.

`"Write about the cultural significance of the Great Wall of China."` (The subject here is "the cultural significance of the Great Wall of China", providing the AI with a clear topic to write about.)

Context: This is not always required, but providing context can help the AI generate a more targeted response. This could involve specifying the audience (e.g., 'for a fifth-grade student'), the format (e.g., 'in bullet points'), the purpose (e.g., 'for a debate'), or the style (e.g., 'in layman's terms').

`"Explain the process of photosynthesis as if you were teaching a group of fifth graders."` (The context is teaching a group of fifth graders, which guides the AI to use simpler, more accessible language.)

Specificity: This could be a particular angle or aspect of the subject you want the AI to focus on. Instead of asking it to 'discuss climate change', you could ask it to 'discuss the impact of climate change on polar wildlife'. This helps prevent the AI from generating too broad or off-topic responses.

"Discuss the impact of the French Revolution specifically on the women's rights movement." (The specificity is "impact of the French Revolution on the women's rights movement", narrowing down the focus of the response.)

Length: This is an indirect way of controlling how detailed you want the response to be. A longer prompt generally encourages a more detailed response, while a shorter prompt is more likely to result in a concise answer.

`"In a short paragraph, summarize the key impacts of the Industrial Revolution."` (The length is specified as "a short paragraph", signaling the AI to provide a concise response.)

Setting the tone:

Setting the tone helps guide the AI's language and sentiment. If you want a humorous response, start your prompt in a light-hearted manner. If you want a serious or academic response, use a more formal tone.

`"In a humorous tone, describe what it's like to work from home."` (The tone here is "humorous", encouraging the AI to take a light-hearted approach.)

Here are some tone examples:

- **Reassuring:**
    - Comforting
    - Soothing
    - Encouraging
    - Supportive
- **Confident:**
    - Assertive
    - Bold
    - Self-assured
    - Strong-willed
- **Informative:**
    - Educational
    - Knowledgeable
    - Fact-based
    - Enlightening
- **Inspirational:**
    - Motivating
    - Empowering

- o Uplifting
- o Visionary

Let's consider a scenario where a person named Alex needs to write an email to his team, encouraging them to meet their project deadline. Alex wants the tone of the email to be motivating but respectful, and he wants to acknowledge the team's hard work so far.

A potential prompt for this could be: `"Write a motivating and respectful email to a team working hard to meet a project deadline, acknowledging their efforts and encouraging them to push through to the finish."`

Here's how this breaks down:

Command: `"Write"` — This is the action that Alex wants the AI to perform, which is to write an email.

Subject: `"a motivating and respectful email to a team working hard to meet a project deadline"` — This tells the AI what the email is about and who the audience is.

Tone: `"motivating and respectful"` — This specifies the desired sentiment of the email.

Context: `"to a team working hard to meet a project deadline"` — This provides additional information about the situation, helping the AI to tailor the email appropriately.

Specificity: `"acknowledging their efforts and encouraging them to push through to the finish"` — This narrows down the main points that Alex wants to communicate in the email.

Plugin recommendation: Download the "Prompt Perfect" plugin.

Link:v https://promptperfect.jina.ai/

The Prompt Perfect plugin is a tool designed to optimize prompts for AI Chatbots such as OpenAI ChatGPT, among others. It has an advanced natural language processing techniches to refine and enhance the prompts. These techniques include sentiment analysis, entity recognition and contextual understanding to optimize the query you provide into very well crafted prompt for the best results.

How does it work?: The tool automates the process of prompt engineering for large language models, but the exact mechanisms or algorithms it uses to achieve this it is not fully provided. The plugin guides the Chatbot to provide responses that align with the intended tone or context. Whatever query you enter, ranging from simple keywords or phrases to complex and structured sentences, it can read the prompt's intent and optimize it to enhance the quality of the AI-generated content, making it more coherent, relevant, and contextually appropriate.

Integrate Keywords Everywhere with ChatGPT

Keywords Everywhere is a browser extension designed to help online marketers, writers and SEO experts. It displays relevant keyword data such as search volume, cost per click, competition and similar keywords in an easy-to-read format. You can integrate this tool with ChatGPT and it can help you with copywriting in your prompts and generate content as well.

The process of integrating this tool with ChatGPT is easy.

Here are the step-by-step instructions:

Step 1: Download the Keywords Everywhere Extension

Keywords Everywhere is available as a browser extension for both Google Chrome and Mozilla Firefox. To download it, navigate to the Keywords Everywhere website or just google "Keywords Everywhere extension". Once you're there click link for your browser of choice. This will take you to the extension's page in your browser's web store. Click on "Add to Chrome" or "Add to Firefox" and confirm any prompts that appear. The extension will then be installed in your browser.

Step 2: Activate the Keywords Everywhere Extension

Once you have the extension installed, you will see a "K" icon in your browser's toolbar. This icon represents Keywords Everywhere. Click on this icon and follow the prompts to set up and activate the extension. You will be asked to agree to the terms of service, and if you wish to access the premium features, you will need to purchase and enter an API key.

Step 3: Use Keywords Everywhere with Your Browser

With the extension activated, you can now start using Keywords Everywhere. Whenever you enter a keyword into your search engine, wherever it is, the extension will automatically provide you with data about that keyword. The data varies, it will show you things like its search volume, cost per click, and competition among other things.

Step 4: Refresh ChatGPT

If you have ChatGPT open in another tab or window or just refresh the page. This ensures that any changes or additions you've made in your browser, like installing the Keywords Everywhere extension, are updated and active in your ChatGPT session.

When you first pull up the ChatGPT screen, you'll see it's pretty straightforward and easy to get around. Over on the left, there's a button that says "Templates". This is your shortcut to a bunch of ready-to-go templates that make it a breeze to work with ChatGPT.

If you give that "Templates" button a click, you'll see a whole bunch of pre-set prompts that help steer the AI to spit out the kind of content you're after. Whether you're looking to draft a news article, brainstorm some ideas, or whip up a product description, these templates are a real-time-saver.

Up at the top of the ChatGPT screen, there are a few dropdown menus labeled "Category", "Subcategory", and "Templates". These help you fine-tune the kind of content you want the AI to generate.

The "Category" dropdown lets you pick the broad type of content you're after, like "Writing", "Learning", or "Brainstorming". Once you've picked a category, you can use the "subcategory" dropdown to get more specific. So if you pick "Writing" as your category, you might see subcategories like "Blog Post", "Product Description", or "Story". This is very useful to write long pieces of content.

The "Templates" dropdown is where you pick a specific prompt template that fits with the category and subcategory you've chosen. These templates give you a jumping-off point for your work with ChatGPT, steering the AI in the direction you want to go.

Over in the top right-hand corner of the screen, there's a button that says "Pls Continue". This gives you even more control over how the

AI keeps generating content. When you click it, you'll see a bunch of options like "Clarify", "Exemplify", "Expand", "Explain", "Rewrite", "Shorten", and "Tweetify". Each of these options tells ChatGPT to handle the next bit of content in a certain way. "Clarify" makes the AI clear up any confusing bits, while "Exemplify" gets it to

give an example. "Expand" tells it to go into more detail, while "Explain" asks for a more in-depth explanation. "Rewrite" has the AI rephrase things, and "Shorten" tells it to cut things down. "Tweetify" gets it to boil things down to a tweet-length message.

All these features together make ChatGPT a really versatile tool that can spit out all kinds of content, all tailored to what you need. So it is very useful as as I mentioned before great for creating long pieces and following up with it. So download it, and start playing around with it so you can get the hand ot it.

Hack # 1 Use The Playground Feature:

https://platform.openai.com/playground

Playground is a web-based platform that you will find in the OpenAI website. As you already know OpenAI is ChatGPT's company. This feature allows users to experiment and interact with OpenAI language models. It is very user-friendly and works in a similar way to ChatGPT, users can input prompts and get a response in real-time.

Understand the differences between Playground and ChatGPT:

Open Playground is a more general platform

ChatGPT is a specific conversation AI model within the platform

They work similar but they are different.

ChatGPT is designed for general use by the public, That's why more people know about the existence of ChatGPT more than Playground. while Playground is more tailored for developers interested in experimenting with OpenAI's various AI technologies.

ChatGPT comes pre-trained and is ready for use right out of the box, meaning it is meant for the masses to use due to its simplicity. This makes it convenient for users who don't have the technical expertise to use AI models. In contrast, OpenAI Playground offers more customizability, allowing developers to tailor AI models to specific needs, so they can customize certain aspects of the type of response they can get.

If you see to the right of the picture above, there are many options to customize the type of response you need, ChatGPT doesn't have any of these. It includes features like the ability to adjust the model's response length, control the randomness of the output, and select from various system personas. These features provide users with additional flexibility and control over the model's behavior to generate responses that align with their preferences or requirements. Playground also allows users to explore and experiment with a variety of machine learning models, including GPT-3, a powerful transformer-based language model.

Make sure you are using your options to the right when using the feature. **Here are what each of them does:**

Mode: The mode feature allows users to choose between two modes of operation: training or inference. Training mode allows users to train a model, while inference mode allows users to interact with a model.

Model: This feature allows you to select the model you want to use, as OpenAI keeps developing new interactive models, more of them will be added to this. Each model has different capabilities, features and uses.

Temperature: The temperature feature allows users to adjust the temperature of the model, meaning the type of diversity in the output you will get. A lower temperature will result in more repetitive text, while a higher temperature will result in more diverse text.

Maximum Length: Self-explanatory, it means the amount of length of words you want for the output.

Spot Sequences: The Spot Sequences feature allows users to specify sequences of text that should be included in the generated text.

Other Features: The Playground also includes additional features such as pre-trained models, datasets, real-time debugging tools, and code snippets.

Playground can work better than ChatGPT for certain things, such as creating interactive conversations. Getting nonbiased responses (For certain things), also Playground has a bit fewer restrictions than ChatGPT.

In summary, the Playground section in OpenAI offers an interactive and user-friendly environment for individuals to experiment with and explore the capabilities of OpenAI's language models and at the same time, customize the type of output you want.

If you have more questions about how the Playground feature works and its differences with ChatGPT you can try these prompts below:

"Could you explain the concept and purpose of OpenAI's Playground feature and explain the differences between the Playground feature on OpenAI and ChatGPT?"

"In detail, how does the Playground feature on OpenAI function?"

"What are the main components of the Playground feature in OpenAI and how do they contribute to its functionality?"

"How does the functionality of OpenAI's Playground compare to ChatGPT?"

"What are the key similarities between ChatGPT and OpenAI's Playground in terms of their operations and capabilities?"

Hack #2: Have ChatGPT Create Prompts For You

This is so straightforward that you probably haven't thought about this. But it is actually one of the most specific ways to have the prompts you need to get the results you want. Just ask it to generate a prompt about a specific subject. This direct approach is often overlooked due to the perceived complexity of AI technology but it can be very simple and effective.

Here are some examples:

"Create prompts for ChatGPT to generate content about how"

"Develop prompts that guide ChatGPT in producing content about..."

"Craft prompts to help ChatGPT generate content related to..."

"Formulate prompts for ChatGPT to create insightful content on..."

```
"Design prompts that will inspire ChatGPT to
generate content focusing on..."
"Compose prompts to lead ChatGPT in creating
content about...
```

The first step is to identify your specific need, ask yourself: Are you looking for in-depth explanations, a list of ideas, a creative story, a critical analysis, or something else? What exactly? If you understand what is exactly you need it will guide you on crafting the correct prompt that will guide ChaGPT to create prompts for you.

Just like we discussed before it needs to be clear, specific and directed towards your goal. All it takes is a direct command. Let's say that you are studying world war II and you need to create content about it, you may say: `"Generate essay prompts to give ChatGPT to generate content about the impact of World War II on global politics."`

You have to make sure you ask Chatgpt to Create prompts **FOR** ChatGPT **TO** generate content about. (FOR.TO)

Example Below:

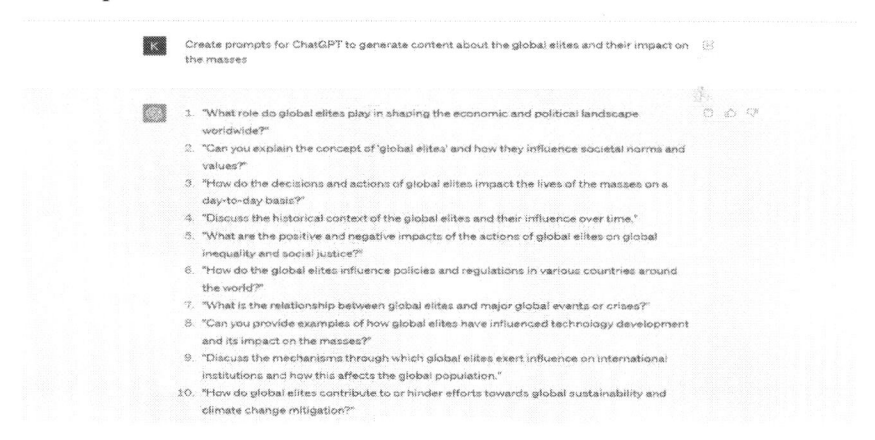

> Create prompts for ChatGPT to generate content about the global elites and their impact on the masses
>
> 1. "What role do global elites play in shaping the economic and political landscape worldwide?"
> 2. "Can you explain the concept of 'global elites' and how they influence societal norms and values?"
> 3. "How do the decisions and actions of global elites impact the lives of the masses on a day-to-day basis?"
> 4. "Discuss the historical context of the global elites and their influence over time."
> 5. "What are the positive and negative impacts of the actions of global elites on global inequality and social justice?"
> 6. "How do the global elites influence policies and regulations in various countries around the world?"
> 7. "What is the relationship between global elites and major global events or crises?"
> 8. "Can you provide examples of how global elites have influenced technology development and its impact on the masses?"
> 9. "Discuss the mechanisms through which global elites exert influence on international institutions and how this affects the global population."
> 10. "How do global elites contribute to or hinder efforts towards global sustainability and climate change mitigation?"

All kinds of people in different circumstances can benefit from this simple approach since this is a great method to have prompts that will help you create content. It works on a variety of subjects and fields, including science, arts, history, technology, you name it. It's as easy as telling ChatGPT to create prompts regarding a particular subject or objective. Practice it yourself and start generating content.

ChatGPT for content creation:

Whatever your industry is, ChatGPT offers countless opportunities for the creation of content. It can act as a collaborator during brainstorming sessions, a copyeditor, a language translator, and so much more. By presenting the topic to the AI, it can stimulate fresh ideas and multiple prompts to expand for a unique, exciting, and engaging piece of content, plus adding your human touch to it, you can easily create a great piece of art.

You can also adjust your writing style very easily and adapt it for different platforms or audiences.

I want to provide just a few examples of what can be created:

- Blog Posts: Brainstorming blog post topics, generating outlines, and even drafting entire posts.
- Emails: ChatGPT can assist in creating acceptable and successful content for emails, whether they are written in a formal tone or a more casual one. Effective subject lines and email signatures can also benefit from it.
- Marketing Content: ChatGPT can create engaging product descriptions, catchy taglines, compelling ad copy for advertising campaigns, persuasive CTA (Call to action), generate SEO-friendly content, etc, overall lots of different digital marketing strategies.
- Scripts: For whatever you need it for: Podcast, video, etc. ChatGPT can help write scripts
- Speeches: It can provide different ways to start or end the speech, suggest anecdotes, or even help in adding humor.
- Social Media Posts: Help generate engaging content for various social media platforms
- Educational Content: Create study materials

Let's take a look at using AI-generated prompts and brainstorming techniques to generate content. As we discussed before, giving the system a few keywords/prompts on topics you will like to explore ChatGPT can help you come up with ideas. The system will generate relevant questions, statements or ideas relevant to topics and if you want to create prompts to generate those topics for you, we already discussed how to do that in Hack#1. This can help you fuel creativity and generate new ideas for content creation in an organized way.

What is brainstorming?

Brainstorming in a traditional sense is when you or a group of people meet up, propose a topic, and people start coming up with different ideas about that topic without any criticism or initial evaluation. The goal is to encourage free thinking, the flow of ideas and spur innovation. With the power of ChatGPT this has been significantly enhanced.

If you are brainstorming alone ChatGPT can act as a virtual partner to you, offering suggestions, expanding different ideas and providing different perspectives that you might not have considered all on your own. ChatGPT doesn't have personal biases or emotions, so it can provide inputs that are free from human prejudices. This can be helpful when you want to explore ideas without being influenced by personal beliefs or opinions. It is not supposed to replace the need for your human creativity and judgment it is just supposed to contribute to the brainstorming process.

Combining these two techniques of using AI-generated prompts and brainstorming can help you create unique content quickly and efficiently. With AI taking care of the basics, you can focus your efforts on refining and expanding the content. You can also use AI to help create a basic outline for the content, which can then be customized and personalized further by humans.

Here are some great 3 steps you can use to create a great piece of content with AI:

Step 1: Create your first draft of content:

For whatever type of content you are creating whether is an email, marketing copy, etc. The creation of a first draft is a critical part of the content creation process. That's how you want to break it down. The first draft helps to get your thoughts down on paper and just get content in. It provides a basis for refining and enhancing your ideas, and serves as a catalyst for further creativity.

Creating a first draft is about moving past the concept of perfection and simply starting to write. It's not so much about getting the words right, but getting your ideas out. The goal is to let the ideas flow and the content in, Don't worry about editing and refining it just yet. Try to write quickly without worrying too much about grammar, punctuation, or style. Avoid editing as you write. This can interrupt your thought process and make it harder to get your ideas down. The editing phase comes later.

Step 2 Refine and Some Edits: Once you are done putting your piece of content together it is time to review and make initial edits, no major edits just yet. You want to focus more on structural issues, Does the piece flow logically? Are there any sections that need to be moved, added, or removed? Are your arguments clear and supported? This is also a good time to flesh out any points that need more detail. By the end of this stage, you should have a fairly solid piece of work.

The revision and editing process can generally be thought of as a multi-step process as well. While you are reading it you can edit it. Check your sentences and paragraphs—are they clear and concise? Are there better words or phrases you could use? Are there any inconsistencies or contradictions? This is a good time to make sure all your facts and figures are correct. By the end of this stage, your piece should be around 80-90% complete.

Step 3 Proofreading/final edit: This is your final pass, where you check for spelling, grammar, and punctuation errors, as well as any minor issues with phrasing or word choice. Reading your work aloud can be particularly useful at this stage, as it can help you catch errors and awkward phrasing that you might overlook when reading silently. By the end of this stage, your work should be polished and ready to publish.

Summarizing:

Step 1: First draft of the content, mildly organized

Step 2: Initial edits, proofreading and organizing it, Adding and removing content getting 70-80 percent ready

Step 3: Final polishing of your content, final edits, humanizing it getting it 100 percent ready for publishing.

Tip: The longer your content is, the more you should probably have a first draft in one document, such as word or google docs, and then do the second and third drafts in a separate document

Here are some prompt examples to come up with ideas for non-fiction content:

```
"Detail the process of starting a … What are
the key steps and considerations?"

"Write a beginner's guide TO …"

"Explain how to set up… What are some
essential tips for beginners?"

"Create a step-by-step guide on how to … What
are the major stages of the process?"

"Provide a guide on how to… What do beginners
need to know?"

"Create a how-to guide on… What are the key
steps, and what makes this recipe special?"

"Write a tutorial on how …. . What are some
practical tips?"

"Explain how TO .... What are the important
considerations and preparations?
```

Dealing with Lengthy and Complicated Prompts:

When it comes to using long prompts to ChatGPT, sometimes are needed and sometimes are not needed. If you only need a short, straightforward question like " How many years a sea turtle can live" short prompts are sufficient. Long prompts can be used when you are in a situation where you need a complex response, so the Chatbot will need more details of your question to be able to generate that response. So the more complexity of an outcome you need, the longer the prompt may need to be.

So you need to take all factors into account for the outcome and the type of response you need, lengthy prompts may take a little longer to create to make sure it is well crafted and has all the necessary information that AI needs for a good response.

When you may need a long prompt:

1. When the conversation requires an understanding of complex topics (such as legal or medical conversations)
2. When you're attempting to ask a detailed question about a particular topic
3. When attempting to create a story with multiple characters and plot points
4. When you're trying to capture the nuances of human conversation, such as sarcasm, humor, emotion, etc.
5. When wanting the model to remember context from previous replies in order to provide more accurate responses

When you may not need to use long prompts:

1. Simple yes/no inquiries
2. Short-answer trivia questions
3. Small talk or casual conversations that don't require detailed responses
4. When the conversation is limited to a single topic

5. Basic customer service inquiries that don't have complex answers required.

2 Hypothetical scenarios for using a long prompt:

A. Let's say you're working on a piece of creative writing—a short story set in a post-apocalyptic world. You want to provide a substantial amount of context for the story, including details about the world, its history, the main characters, among other things

In this case, a longer prompt would be beneficial, as it allows you to provide the AI with all the necessary information in one go. For instance:

"Write a short story set in a post-apocalyptic world where the majority of humanity lives underground due to a devastating solar event a century ago. The story should center around a protagonist named Alex, a skilled mechanic who stumbles upon a mysterious device that could potentially restore the surface world. The narrative should convey themes of hope, resilience, and discovery."

Using a long prompt is most useful when you are providing detailed instructions or information to the user. When you are trying to explain how a complex process works using a longer prompt can help provide all of the necessary details without having to break them up into multiple shorter prompts, it makes things easier on yourself.

B. You are a student, and you need to write an essay on The cost of US healthcare compared to their countries.

"Please compose a persuasive essay debating the current high cost of health care in the United States compared to other nations.You

should use evidence from reliable sources to support your position, and present a clear and concise argument that will be convincing to the reader. Consider counter-arguments and refute them effectively. Additionally, ensure that your essay is well-organized and uses effective rhetoric. Lastly, make sure to include proper citations and check for spelling and grammar"

All the points being used:

1. Compose a persuasive essay **debating** the current **high cost of health care** in the United States **compared** to other nations.
2. Use **evidence from reliable sources** to support your position.
3. Present a **clear and concise argument**.
4. **Consider counter-arguments and refute** them effectively.
5. Ensure that your **essay is well-organized** and uses effective rhetoric.
6. Include proper citations and **check for spelling** and grammar.

As you see the outcome you needed from the AI was complex so the prompt needed to be longer as a result. You will see that after you create a prompt like that, the Chatbot will guide you a comprehensive guide with all of points you requested. As you see, long prompts should be used when you need to provide a substantial amount of context or al ist of instructions for the AI to generate a comprehensive response.

CHAPTER 4

BRING AI INTO EVERYWHERE YOU WORK

AI in daily lives and business:

Regardless of your work, lifestyle, career, profession or status. AI has the potential to impact virtually every aspect of your life. ChatGPT offers countless benefits you could use if you apply them to your life, work, and routine. As time goes on, AI-driven technologies will become even more pervasive, it will get easier and easier to use, and people will be able to effortlessly interact with machines and easily access information from any divide or location.

Many experts and researchers in the field of AI agree that AI technologies will continue to advance and become even more integrated into our lives by 2030 and beyond. They foresee AI playing a larger role in various sectors, including healthcare, transportation, education, entertainment, and business. The rate of change in the world will continue to accelerate in large part to these advancements in technology, specifically AI technology.

As it continues to become more sophisticated and integrated into our lives, its potential to positively impact us will continue to grow. If we start embracing this technology early, we can create a brighter future for ourselves, everyone around us, and generations to come, you can have AI make your life easier, safer, and more enjoyable as you create a better future for yourself. This Chapter will go over how to apply this versatile tool and a multitude of contexts, from personal day-to-day tasks to complex projects.

You are probably wondering how to start adapting to this little by little in the situation that you are in right now. Well, you know better than us what your life is looking like at the moment, your goal is to use it to your benefit, so you have to adapt accordingly,

As we mentioned at the beginning of the book ChatGPT can help pretty much anyone:

- **Professionals:** AI can boost efficiency, decision-making and improve productivity. I can also facilitate communication by helping you write different pieces of text that relates to your profession.
- **Students:** As we will dive in a little later in the book, AI can help you enhance your study and learning by assisting you in understanding complex topics. AI can easily adapt to individual learning styles, making education more effective and fun.
- **9-to-5 Workers:** there is a wide variety of roles that can benefit from understanding and utilizing AI, while some others might not be as significantly affected, of course, depending on their work.
- **Freelancers:** We made a whole section earlier in the book how freelancers can use ChatGPT
- **Business Owners:** As we discussed earlier as well AI can help business owners take their business to the next level
- **Parents:** Parents can highly benefit by personalized advice and providing engaging learning experiences for kids.
- **Educators:** Teachers, professors, and trainers can use AI to personalize instruction, automate grading, and identify student learning trends. They need to stay on top.

- **Scientists and Researchers:** One of the best tools researchers can have. AI can enhance and speed up the research process
- **Travelers:** AI can help travelers plan trips, navigate new locations, and overcome language barriers.
- **Job Seekers:** AI can help individuals find job opportunities that match their skills and interests, and can even assist in resume building and interview preparation.

You purchased this book with a keen awareness that there's a great deal you're yet to discover. You've recognized that ChatGPT, more than a mere tool, can serve as a supportive companion as you navigate your interests and your path towards your desired lifestyle. The goal here is to enhance your existing capabilities, streamline your tasks, and, overall, simplify your life.

Keep the following things in mind during your adaptation:

Determine Your Needs: You have both personal and professional responsibilities every day. Do you find any tasks in your day-to-day life that can be automated? Maybe you spend considerable time drafting emails, compiling reports, or creating written content work for or school. Think about where AI can enhance your work.

Understand the Tool: If you made it until this point you should have a solid understanding of AI and ChatGPT already. You should have taken the time to engage with it. Prompt it with questions, and observe the responses. The more you interact with ChatGPT, the better you'll understand its abilities and uses and ideas will flow better in where and how to adapt it to get things done.

Tailor It to Your Situation: With a firm grasp of ChatGPT's capabilities, you can now adapt it to your unique needs. If you're a student, it could clarify challenging concepts, assist with homework, or generate study notes. Professionals could leverage it to draft emails, create reports, or brainstorm ideas. The essence lies in adapting the tool to your specific circumstances.

Iterate and Improve: Every tool comes with its learning curve, and ChatGPT is no exception. It might occasionally misinterpret your prompts or produce content not entirely in line with your expectations. Persist in your exploration, refining your prompts and honing your approach. Gradually, your proficiency with ChatGPT will enhance, increasing its value to you.

Stay Open to New Possibilities: The AI landscape is ever-evolving, with constant enhancements to tools like ChatGPT. Stay receptive to these changes, integrating them into your interaction with the tool. Future updates might augment ChatGPT's contextual understanding or creative prowess. Keeping abreast of these advancements empowers you to continuously augment your productivity and efficiency.

You may have noticed that we not only cover how to use ChatGPT but also help you understand the power of AI and how has the ability to transform every aspect of your life. As more and more AI tools will keep coming and AI keeps will keep being integrated into every aspect of life you will see that it is just a matter of time until you will forced to adapt. But when you are forced to adapt you are not going to be able to see as many rewards as the early adopters. In the near future is going to be normal to see people to make everyday tasks easier.

Writing with AI:

We may not realize it but we are constantly writing in this modern world to communicate and work. We often find ourselves writing emails, reports, blog post, work related communication, texts, etc. It has become a normal part of our daily lives. Let alone students where they have to constantly be writing pieces of text for school work. You already know that when it comes to writing, ChatGPT is going to be your best friend. It can help with grammar and spellchecks, it can provide content for you, insights on how to improve your work, generate topics ideas, and many more things. You can enhance your writing skills making your writing more effective, engaging and accurate, AI-powered assistance can also assist with plagiarism detection, suggesting sources for citation if needed as well as providing real-time advice on word choice and sentence structure.

A Tool, Not a Replacement:

It is important to emphasize that AI should be used as a writing assistance and not the finished product, it should not replace your creativity, insight and human judgment. It is supposed to assist you in the creation of content generation and writing assistance, but the final shape of your writing should always come from you.

To get the most out of your writing, just tell ChatGPT exactly what you want it and how you want it., as we talked about before, it all comes down to being specific in your requests. The features of ChatGPT goes beyond just creating text from scratch, if you give it a specific request and follow up to perfect the style, Chatgpt can modify and critique your work

In the following sections, I am going to provide you with different examples of ways you can format such commands depending on the outcome you are looking for. This section is going to be a little different than the prompt section you read earlier, this will be focused more on writing great pieces of content for your work rather than crafting prompts which we already covered.

Including the following elements in your writing commands:

- The specific action you want it to perform (write, edit, critique)
- The topic or content focus
- Any specific details or guidelines related to the task (e.g., the format, style, or tone of the content)
- The target audience, if applicable

Be specific, clear, and guide the AI towards the kind of output you want.

Now, let's look at some examples of such commands:

1. Storytelling:

    a. Generic: "Write a short story."

Specific: "Write a short suspense story set in Victorian England where the main character is a female detective."

    b. Generic: "Write a fantasy story."

Specific: "Write a fantasy story about a young dragon who can't breathe fire trying to find his place in a dragon-dominated society."

2. Blog Writing:

    a. Generic: "Write a blog post."

Specific: "Write a 1000-word blog post about the advantages of veganism for personal health and the environment."

    b. Generic: "Write about technology trends."

Specific: "Write an informative blog post discussing the top 5 technology trends expected to dominate in 2023 and their potential impact on businesses."

3. Research Papers:

    a. **Generic:** "Write a research paper."

Specific: "Write an abstract for a research paper studying the correlation between lack of sleep and cognitive performance in young adults."

b. **Generic:** "Write about climate change."

Specific: "Write a research paper introduction discussing the effects of climate change on the global bee population."

Here are some command templates you can use to guide ChatGPT:

- "Explain [topic]": You can use this to get a detailed explanation of a specific subject. For example, "Explain quantum physics."
- "Write it in [style]": This command directs the AI to write in a certain style. For instance, "Write it in a Shakespearean style."
- "Describe [subject]": This prompt helps in getting detailed descriptions. For example, "Describe a bustling city at dawn."
- "Summarize [text/topic]": You can use this command to get a concise summary. For instance, "Summarize the plot of 'War and Peace.'"
- "Rewrite this [sentence/paragraph] in [tone]": This guides the AI to rewrite a piece of text with a certain tone. For example, "Rewrite this paragraph in a humorous tone."
- "Critique this [piece of writing]": This command prompts the AI to provide feedback on a specific piece of writing. For instance, "Critique this introduction."
- "Create a [type of content] about [topic]": This is useful for generating specific types of content. For example, "Create a poem about spring."
- "Make this [more/less] [specific characteristic]": This command guides the AI to edit a text according to a special characteristic
- Write this for [specific audience]

Be flexible on how specific you are especially if you need to be broad, this is particularly important if you need to leave room for the AI to come up with an original and insightful response

For example:

Too vague: `"Write about dogs."`

Just right: `"Write a short informative article about the benefits of adopting rescue dogs, focusing on their resilience and adaptability."`

Too specific: `"Write an article about the benefits of adopting rescue dogs, mentioning that they are generally mixed breeds, which means they are healthier, and then talk about how they're already trained, and finally discuss how adopting a rescue dog is a good way to give a second chance to an animal that has been abandoned."`

The "just right" version guides the AI toward a specific topic and angle (the benefits of adopting rescue dogs, focusing on resilience and adaptability) but doesn't prescribe exactly what points it should make, allowing it to generate a more unique response.

Remember, this balance may vary depending on the context and what you're trying to achieve. Experimentation is key to find what works best for your particular needs.

Rephrasing and Paraphrasing:

Rephrasing and paraphrasing are two different techniques used to reword written content in order to make it clearer or more concise. Both consist on rewriting pieces in content in a different way that is more understandable. Rephrasing involves taking a statement, passage or piece of text and recasting it using different words while keeping the same meaning, on the other hand, paraphrasing involves completely rewriting the original piece of content with your own words while still conveying the same message. Rephrasing stands for rewriting something to make it clearer and much easier to comprehend, Paraphrasing, slightly different, means changing an original thought into a new one the way YOU understood it. If you are going to be using AI to generate content, you will need to know what these two are and how to do this since AI detectors will be there waiting for you.

Paraphrasing will require a deep understanding of the text, it is not just about changing words, but also comprehending the piece of text, restructuring sentences and organize the ideas in a way that "clicked" with you so it can click with someone else the same way. (Your audience)

When it comes to using ChatGPT to do these, this is crucial for several reasons, first the more people use AI, and it gets integrated in our daily lives, the more people will be able to tell AI content from human-generated content, and when people see that you use AI to completely write your piece of text without adding a human touch to it it will turn a lot of people off. Human-like content will be highly reworded. It will be a while until AI is able to write things completely in a human like way. You need to humanize your content for people to connect to it on a human level.

Secondly, by learning to rephrase and paraphrase, you can ensure accuracy as well as clarity to of the message being conveyed, this can ensure not only that people will connect with your writing but also that they can understand it.

Rephrasing example:

- **Original text:**

Credit cards are types of payment cards that allow you to borrow money from a bank on a short-term basis. When you make purchases with a credit card, you are essentially borrowing money from the card issuer and then paying it back with interest over time. Building a good credit score is important because it shows lenders that you are a responsible borrower and can be trusted with money. A good credit score can also help you to secure better loan terms, credit cards, and other financial products.

- **Rephrased text:**

Credit cards is a way to borrowing money. Basically you take out a short-term loan from a bank. When you use a credit card to make purchases, you are essentially borrowing money from the company that issued the card and gradually repaying it with interest. Being able to borrow money responsibly and be trusted with it is demonstrated by having a high credit score, which is crucial to lenders. You can obtain better loan conditions, credit card offers, and other financial goods with a high credit score.

As you see both are similar, but they are lightly reworded for you to comprehend it a bit easier.

There are a lot of different writing styles that allow you to fit different types of audiences, convey a message in an effective way and bring clarity to a subject or topic. For example, if you are writing for a technical audience, using technical language can help make your points clear and concise. Writing styles also play an important role in helping readers understand and engage with what you've written, you can use elements such as rhetoric and persuasion techniques, and writing styles can create interesting pieces that capture the interest of their readers.

Here are a few examples of different writing styles and a short description of them :

Conversational Writing: This style mimics spoken language. It's typically casual, using simpler sentences and everyday vocabulary. You can ask ChatGPT to rephrase content in a conversational style, which can be useful for blog posts or social media content.

Descriptive Writing: This style focuses on providing detailed descriptions of people, places, objects, or events, using sensory language to create vivid imagery and engage the reader's senses.

Persuasive Writing: This style aims to persuade or convince the reader to adopt a particular viewpoint or take a specific action. It employs persuasive techniques, logical reasoning, and evidence to support the writer's position.

Narrative Writing: This style involves storytelling and typically follows a chronological sequence of events. It aims to engage the reader by presenting a narrative with characters, settings, and a plot.

Creative Writing: This style is characterized by the use of figurative language, imagery, and narrative structures. You can ask ChatGPT to rephrase text in a creative or poetic style for writing stories, poems, or scripts.

There is a lot more, and you can research them to find the description of how they work

There are just so many different writing styles that you can use to rephrase a text you have created. Here are **some more:**

- Expository Writing
- Descriptive Writing
- Persuasive Writing
- Narrative Writing
- Argumentative Writing
- Compare and Contrast Writing
- Cause and Effect Writing
- Definition Writing
- Problem/Solution Writing
- Process Writing
- Critical Writing
- Reflective Writing
- Analytical Writing
- Report Writing
- Review Writing
- Abstract Writing
- Satirical Writing
- Epistolary Writing

- Stream of Consciousness Writing
- Dramatic Writing
- Speculative Writing
- Didactic Writing
- Autobiographical Writing
- Script Writing
- Blog Writing
- SEO Writing
- News Writing
- Editorial Writing
- Column Writing
- Feature Writing
- Investigative Writing
- Historical Writing
- Scientific Writing

These are just a few examples to help you understand how different writing styles have different tone with your writing. ChatGPT can help you with this by providing prompts to modify your piece of this in one of these desired styles.

Here are some 2 simple steps I use to to rephrase and paraphrase pieces of text with ChatGPT

Step 1: Provide and command ChatGPT to rephrase or paraphrase

Provide the text you want to paraphrase to ChatGPT and ask to paraphrase the provided in your desired style.

Make your command as explicit as possible. For example, you might say,

```
"Paraphrase the following text in an academic writing style," or "Can you rephrase this in a more conversational tone?"
```

Step 2: Review and Refine the Output

ChatGPT will respond with a paraphrased version of your text in the requested style. Review the output. If it's not quite what you wanted, don't hesitate to ask ChatGPT to try again or to provide the output in a slightly different style. You can refine your command by providing more specifics or adjusting your request.

Here are ten examples of prompts to request ChatGPT to rephrase something in a different style:

- Paraphrase this text in a formal academic style.
- Rephrase this sentence to sound more casual and conversational.
- Provide a paraphrase for the following quote in an old English style.
- Rewrite the following sentence in a more poetic style..
- Can you rephrase this sentence in a more professional tone?
- Rewrite the following text in a more humorous style.
- Paraphrase the following proverb in a modern, slang-heavy style.
- Rephrase the following dialogue as if it was written in a Victorian-era novel.
- Rewrite this technical instruction in a language suitable for children.

It is important to do this because as time goes on and AI becomes more prevalent in society, so will AI detectors. 100 percent AI-generated content will be punished by most online platforms, the SEO may not work as well, different accounts may be subject to penalties such as removal, and you can suffer things like reduced visibility, lack of credibility, or even account suspension.

Rephrasing and paraphrasing must be done ethically and responsibly. Merely replacing words or rearranging sentence patterns just to avoid AI detectors without adding your own input of general content can still backfire on you because these minor changes can still be detected. Sometimes the best way to rephrase a AI-generated text is to do it yourself. You will notice that rephrasing AI text with AI will still not get around these detractors. When you are making big claims make sure you provide your sources, stay updated with the policies and guidelines of the platform you are using and add your own human touch with every piece of content you create, this will help you from keeping you from being banned, and to people with connect with your writing.

You have to Fact-Check your outputs:

You have to fact-check ChatGPT responses. Especially if you are a student. You will find that more often than it should, the AI will provide inaccurate information, and you have to make sure that information is correct. One simple way of doing that is by directly asking follow-up questions or seeking additional sources of information. , or just Asking ChatGPT to fact-check it.

Here are some prompt examples that can help you fact-check:

- "Please fack check this"
- "Can you provide a source or reference for that information?"
- "How did you arrive at that conclusion? Could you explain the reasoning or evidence behind it?"
- "Is there any research or study that supports this claim?"
- "Are there any alternative viewpoints or conflicting evidence on this topic?"
- "Can you provide specific examples or case studies to back up your statement?"

AI models are highly sophisticated, but they haven't got the point of human reasoning just yet, it doesn't truly *"understand"* the content they generate. Instead, they learn patterns and correlations from the data they were trained on and use these patterns to generate new text.

This means that they can inadvertently produce incorrect or misleading information sometimes. So It lacks subject matter expertise and lacks specialized education to understand common sense, judgment and human experience, so you should fact check especially when given professional-related information like medical, law, or sophisticated scientific topics.

Humanizing AI Generated Content:

While AI can guide our pens, it is the human heart that breathes life into words.

This goes in hand with the previous section, but it is worth mentioning a few things.

AI is a great tool that can help us in the process of writing, it is critical to remember that it should not replace the human element in writing.

Content that connects with readers on a human level often carries more impact. It's the unique human perspective, emotion, humor, and understanding of complex social and cultural contexts that make content truly engaging and relatable. AI-generated text is still quite new, and people may not recognize it as well now, but in just a free years, it will be a different story. By humanizing your content, you wil be able to connect to humans because, after all humans will be reading what you are writing, you have to add that human touch. People will notice a lack of personal touch, emotion, humor, or deep understanding of complex subjects in AI-written text. Although it is expected that as AI technologies continue to advance, we might expect them to become better at mimicking human writing styles. In some cases, they might already produce text that's hard to distinguish from human-written content, but I am sure we are years away from that. You still want to humanize your content as much as possible, it will always be more valuable than copying and pasting AI-generated content without putting your own input into it.

Now you may be wondering how you humanize. Here are some ways:

We have discovered that you can use humanizing prompts, and the AI will do a good job in making the text sound more human, but it is still caught by AI detectors. Sometimes the best practice is to read it yourself and writing it in your own words while you read it. You may need to use two different monitors while you read in one and write in the other, this makes it a lot easier. It all depends on what you are going to be using the content for, If you use it for marketing, sales funnels, and places where you are not going to be checked for AI content, you should be ok using rephrasing tools like Quillbot or rephrasing prompts. But if you are going to be using it for website content, study-related material or putting your content to be read on the internet, you may be penalized for using AI.

AI-Generated Content: Situations where it's ok to use and where you can be penalized for it

Generally penalized for using AI-generated content:

- Academia: This is the most obvious. Most colleges or universities will penalize you for it, it would be considered academic dishonesty (similar to plagiarism). Which most likely will result in severe penalties, such as failing grades, suspension, or even expulsion.
- Journalism and Publishing: Many journalistic and publishing entities maintain strict standards for authenticity and originality. If a journalist were to use AI-generated content without attribution or disclosure, it could result in job loss or damaged reputation.
- Legal proceedings: In the context of legal proceedings, presenting AI-generated content as genuine or human-created could be considered fraudulent, potentially leading to serious legal consequences. Like even losing licences
- Plagiarism and Copyright Infringement: D o not use AI to plagiarize or infringe upon someone else's intellectual property rights.

Places where is generally ok to use AI-generated content:

- **Marketing and Sales:** AI-generated content is commonly used in marketing campaigns, sales funnels, and email marketing to drive conversions. Typically for things like running ads, there are no AI detectors that will penalize your work.
- **Entertainment Industry:** Very common. AI-generated content finds application in the entertainment industry, including gaming, film, and television. It can be used to generate realistic characters, dialogue, and even entire storylines, adding new dimensions to creative productions.
- **AI Research and Development:** AI-generated content is extensively used in AI research and development, allowing researchers to train and improve algorithms, explore new applications, and advance the capabilities of artificial intelligence.
- **Content Generation Tools:** Online platforms and software with AI-powered content generation tools enable users to automate content creation processes, such as generating articles, blog posts, and social media updates, improving efficiency and productivity.
- **Creative Expression and Artistic Projects:** AI-generated content offers artists and creators new avenues for expression. It can be used in music composition, visual art, and creative writing, facilitating unique and experimental approaches to artistic endeavors.

Humanizing options and tips:

1. **Rephrase and paraphrase yourself:** AI may sometimes generate overly formal or structured sentences. Reviewing and revising the text to be more conversational can help. For example, instead of "It is highly recommended that the user reboot the system," you might say "You should try rebooting your system."

AI-generated text: "It is suggested that individuals find hobbies that can help distract them from stressors."

Humanized version: *"Why not find a hobby you love? It's a great way to take your mind off what's stressing you out."*

Once you have your second draft where you information is all well organized, while you read it and do final edits is when you can humanize by basically using your own brain, Rephrasing tools can do a good job as well, but they are still caught by AI detectors that can hurt you in the long run.

2. **Check for Coherence:** AI can occasionally produce content that lacks coherence or logical flow, especially over long stretches of text. Review the content for coherence and reorder points or paragraphs if necessary to ensure the text flows smoothly from one idea to the next.

    AI-generated text: "Exercise is beneficial. Mindfulness reduces stress. Sleep is important."

    While these sentences are factually correct, they lack coherence as they are presented as isolated ideas.

    Humanized version: "Exercise, mindfulness, and a good night's sleep are all interconnected pieces of the puzzle in managing stress effectively."

    In the humanized version, the three elements are tied together into a coherent, single thought about stress management.

3. **Personalize Content:** Adding personal anecdotes, experiences, or examples can make the text more relatable. AI-generated text often lacks a personal touch as it doesn't have personal experiences. After the AI generates the text, you can inject some of your own experiences to make it more human.

AI-generated text: "Dealing with stress involves a combination of good nutrition, exercise, and quality sleep."

Humanized version: "I remember when stress was taking over my life – the sleepless nights and constant worries. But over the years, I've found a mix of good nutrition, regular exercise, and a quality sleep schedule to be my personal recipe for managing stress."

4. **Adjust the Tone:** Make sure the tone of the text aligns with the context and audience. A professional document will have a different tone than a blog post for a general audience. An AI might not always get the tone right, so adjusting it can make the text more suitable and human.

AI-generated text: "The implementation of relaxation techniques can assist in the mitigation of stress."

Humanized version: "Hey, guess what? Using relaxation techniques can really help chill out those stress levels."

Also, when you are humanizing, read it out loud while doing edits; this helps identify whether the language used sounds natural and helps identify areas that need improvement. Make it sound like a human wrote it, add your own input, and revise the sentences that are too structured to make it sound more natural. AI should only assist you in the first phases when you crafting a well-put-together piece of content and as the human you are, you give your content "life".

The goal of this are multiple: Making sure the final text we create reads as it came from a human rather than an automated system, not having problems with our content being punished by AI detectors online, and connect with our readers on a human level.

Here are some examples of Humanizing prompts you could use but keep in mind that while they can do a good job in making AI-generated text sound more human, they probably still won't pass AI detectors:

- "I have this piece of text that seems a bit stiff and robotic. Could you please rephrase it to make it sound more natural and human-like?"
- "This text doesn't feel very human. Can you help me rewrite it to sound more like a conversation between friends?"
- "Could you please help me paraphrase this text in a way that makes it sound less formal and more like everyday speech?"
- "I need to humanize this text. Can you rephrase it to make it sound less like it was written by an AI and more like a person wrote it?"
- "I want this text to feel more natural and less like it came from a machine. Could you help me rewrite it to achieve that?"
- "Can you help me reword this text? I'd like it to sound less mechanical and more human."
- "This text needs a bit of human touch. Can you help me rewrite it in a way that it doesn't sound like it was written by an AI?"

Hack #3: Use The Browsing Beta In ChatGPT4:

Browsing beta is a feature/Plugin. This allows ChatGPT to analyze web links in the ways you ask for. This is a significant step to be able to use ChatGPT with more updated information and not just the cut-off date in 2021. This allows you to obtain whatever information you want about whatever link you give it. It allows the AI to access websites with easy access, such as blogs, and analyzes the content you ask and provides responses. It can respond to a variety of different prompts and has different features, like being able to distinguish a display pop-up window from the original content of the website.

The way you use it is very simple. You have to include your prompt/query and your link in the same input. Example:

"Could you please analyze this blog post and summarize the key points?

https://example.com/blog-post"

When you are providing your query and your URL together you're ensuring that the model has a clear understanding of what is needs to do with the link.

Adding the feature to ChatGPT is very easy:

1. Open the Account page of your ChatGPT account and click on the "Settings" tab.
2. On the App Settings page, scroll down to the 'Web Browsing' section and click button to activate.
3. After activating the Web browsing, you will be asked to create a new chat session.

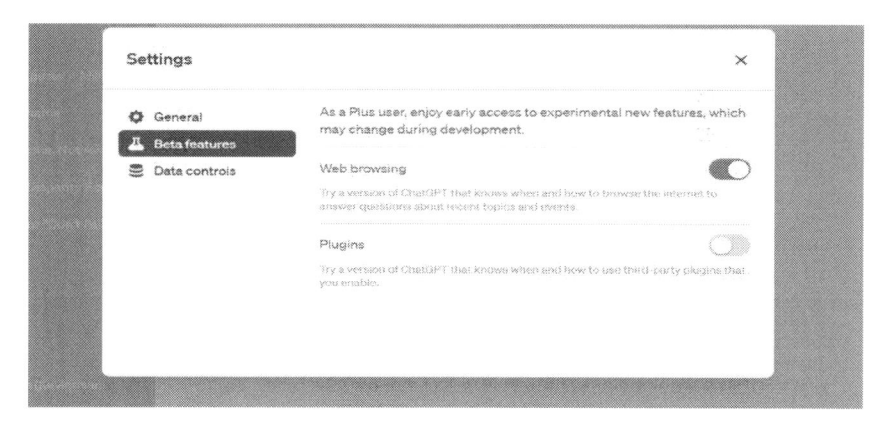

It may look different by the time you are reading this book but it should be something similar.

The Browsing Beta function is able to comprehend lengthy sentences, such as those on lengthy blog sites or Wikipedia pages. It is intended to attempt the desired action multiple times, assuring delivery. The majority of webpage types, including those with text, images, videos, and audio files, may be understood by browsing beta. It makes mistakes on pages that require logging in or have non-textual material. A URL with several links can also be processed by the function without any problems. You will notice that the analysis takes time, and it could take a little longer in situations with large or heavy content. It struggles with webpages that require a login and those with non-textual content such as images, videos, or audio files.

In cases of extensive or heavy content, the analysis might take a little longer.

When it comes to the information that Browsing Beta can provide, the list is extensive. It includes anything related to the content of the web link, allowing the user to receive a wide array of responses. For instance, it can analyze an Amazon link and provide information related to a specific product's niche.

You can use this plugin to help you in your income-generation journey by analyzing trend data analysis, customer behavior, and competitor analysis, among other things that you could use it in your industry.

Hack # 4 Get Advice In Your Particular Situation

You may be surprised that if you provide ChatGPT with a well-crafted prompt explanation of your situation, the AI can give you well-personalized advice to help you in your situation. If you vie your input enough information for the ChatGPT system to understand the general context of the situation, it will interact with you and ask questions to clarify and provide constructive advice in the form of a conversation.

This is a great way to get personalized advice for whatever situation that you are going thru. The responses that the AI tool can provide are intended to be natural, beneficial, and thorough. The system will consider the input, and based on it, it will provide insights and solutions, so the more precise your explanation, the better. ChatGPT will ask you to clarify if it does not comprehend your explanation.

Use it when you are unsure about something, you can apply it to anything:

- Moving to a new city
- Starting a new business
- Starting a new relationship
- Career change
- Financial difficulties
- Conflict resolution
- Dealing with Anxiety
- Adjusting to a new job
- Balancing work and personal life
- Planning a major event
- Starting a new job
- Going through a breakup
- Planning a vacation
- Dealing with a difficult coworker
- Becoming a parent for the first time

These are just a few of the things you can get personalized advice for.

It is quite likely that the use of AI for personalized advice will continue to grow more common and accepted. The AI will be able to take into account everything that you say it and offer advice that's tailored to the specific person and context. Also can be accessed 27/7 from virtually anywhere, it can learn from each interaction and as AI will keep improving this feature will be refined. People also will feel comfortable discussing sensitive topics or personal issues with AI more than with a person.

Tips, Advise Request and Prompt examples:

Tip 1: You need to provide clear and precise details about the current situation you're in, and provide enough supporting evidence to help ChatGPT understand the context.

Prompt 1: "I'm in a management position in a tech company and my team of five software engineers is having a problem with meeting deadlines. They're very talented, but they tend to underestimate the time required for their tasks, which leads to delays. This has been going on for the last six months despite our efforts to improve estimation skills. How can I help my team improve in this area?"

Tip 2: Once you are in the conversation. Include relevant information about potential solutions and any relevant actions that are available to you.

Prompt 2: "I am a college student majoring in psychology and I'm having trouble deciding between pursuing a career in clinical psychology or educational psychology. I have interned in a clinic last summer and found it rewarding but also quite challenging. I've also had a part-time job as a teaching assistant at a school, which I enjoyed. I have the opportunity to intern at a school psychology department next semester. Can you help me weigh the pros and cons of both career paths?"

Tip 3: Present only one issue or decision with as much clarity as possible. This will help ChatGPT understand the whole story more easily.

Prompt 3: "I'm a small business owner selling handmade soaps and body care products. I've been using social media for advertising, but I'm unsure if I should invest in paid advertisements to reach a wider audience. My budget is limited, but I can allocate some funds for marketing. Should I continue with organic growth or invest in paid advertisements?"

Tip 4: Remain open-minded: Even though you might have a specific question in mind, ChatGPT might provide an answer or solution that you had not thought of.

Prompt 4: "I'm an aspiring novelist struggling with writer's block. I've tried setting a writing schedule, finding a quiet place to write, and even changing my writing tools. Still, nothing seems to work. Do you have any advice?"

Tip 5: Consider presenting multiple potential scenarios to provide ChatGPT with more information so that it can provide a better response.

Prompt 5: "I am a newly appointed project manager at a software development company. We have a crucial project that is behind schedule. I've thought of two potential solutions: (1) Overwork the team to catch up, but risk burning them out or (2) Ask for an extension from the client, but risk damaging our professional relationship. What are your thoughts on these options, or do you suggest an alternative approach?"

Here are more examples in the area you can get personalized advice:

Career Choices:

"What could be the potential outcomes if I decide to shift my career from corporate law to nonprofit work?"

"I am currently working as a graphic designer but I'm thinking of transitioning into UI/UX design. What might be the implications of this career change?"

"What if I choose to pursue a career in academia after spending several years in the tech industry? What challenges and opportunities might I face?"

Business Decisions:

"I am considering expanding my local retail business to an online platform. What might be the benefits and challenges of this transition?"

"What if I invest in the real estate market instead of sticking to my current investment portfolio in stocks? What kind of risks and potential gains could I expect?"

"I'm thinking about franchising my successful coffee shop. What could be the implications of this decision on my business?"

Life Paths:

"What might my life look like if I decide to take a year off work to travel around the world?"

```
"I'm considering going back to school to get
a master's degree in my mid-30s. How might
this   decision   affect   my   personal   and
professional life?"

"What if I decide to move from a big city to
a  rural  area?  What  lifestyle  changes  can  I
anticipate?"
```

Now keep in mind it is not intended to replace professional advice. Particularly in areas that demand specialist knowledge, such as legal affairs, healthcare, and other expert-led domains, the guidance provided by ChatGPT should be considered as supplemental at most. For example, it could provide preliminary insights or general perspectives, but it cannot substitute the nuanced and detailed advice provided by trained professionals in these fields. It's a complementary tool, not a standalone solution, and should be used accordingly.

Use this feature when it comes to helping you **find a business** in your **specific situation:**

Personalized business selection advice steps:

Describe who you are to the AI: Explain to ChatGPT the kind of person you are, such as personality traits age, values and other aspects of your identity that could help the AI identify the type of business or side hustle that may fit with your personality.

Explain in which life stage are you: Explain the type of job you have at the moment, if you're studying, how much time you have during the week and other related information like how much money you have, etc. This helps the AI understand the context in which you are looking to start a business.

Explain your skills and interest: Share with ChatGPT your skills and interests to help ChatGPT understand what something that you would understand and enjoy doing is. You can also Specify the type of business you would be interested in starting if you have an idea. Remember that these steps are just a starting point; you might need to provide more information or clarify some points based on the AI's responses. The goal is to have a conversation and follow up, you may want to try to generate a long prompt at once, here is an example where you can use the following fill-in-the-blank prompt:

I am a _____ year old with a personality that is best described as _____. My values and passions include _____.

Currently, I am working as a ___, and I can dedicate around _____ hours per week to a new project. I have a budget of $ that I am ready to invest into starting a small business or side hustle.

My skills and experiences are in _____, and I have a particular interest in _____ and _____.

Based on this, can you suggest some business ideas that align with my skills, interests, available time, and financial resources?"

You can edit this and tailor it to whatever specific thing you would like to add. After providing all of this information, you will get different types of recommendations. We already went over business assessment and selection in Chapter 2.

Hack#5: Download the WebChatGPT Extension

The "WebChatGPT" extension tool is a plugin that allows you to have ChatGPT read the internet for your prompts. So basically, it uses the internet to get responses along with the integrated data. So This allows for more accurate and up-to-date conversations. The extension works by searching up to 10 websites from Google search results that are relevant to your prompt and adding the obtained information to your responses. The extension is compatible with Chrome and Edge (Both Microsoft) . The key difference between using this plugin and not using it lies in the accuracy and up-to-dateness of the information provided.

Without the extension, ChatGPT relies solely on the information it was trained on, which goes up to September 2021, to generate responses. But with the WebChatGPT extension, the model has access to more current information, which allows it to generate responses that are more relevant to the present.

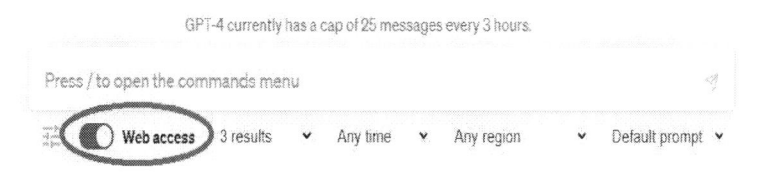

So basically, it gets very close to begin "ChatGPT with internet". After learning everything that you have learned so far with this book, I am sure you will find interesting uses for it. It can help you with business discovery, market analysis, it call pull data from various sources online to identify trends, help you understand the competitive landscape, analyze reviews, and so many other things where a whole book about it can be written

CHAPTER 5

LEARNING SMARTER

AI-Assisted Learning

This chapter is going to be all about using this AI tool for learning. You should always be learning new things. The system allows people to ask questions about subjects they are having trouble understanding and receive clear answers. If you learn how to use ChatGPT for learning which you will in this chapter you can learn things in a fraction of the time that it would take you to look it up somewhere else.

You can easily adapt ChatGPT to a personalised learning that works for you. Personal learning is about tailoring educational content to your individual needs. Basically you are adapting the system to learn in a way that works for you and at your own pace, style and level of understanding.

You are going to start by giving up prompts to the system about the subjects you need to learn about. There are a number of words or phrases to use that can help improve learning and you can give it to the chatbot to enhance and help your understanding of a topic. Practicing this process will enhance your cognitive abilities which are escential for in depth learning and understanding.

To summarize I am going to give you words to use that will help your learning process.

- Define
- Describe
- Explain
- Clarify
- Exempify
- Compare
- Summarize
- Analyze
- Evaluate
- Critique

Here are a few examples:

Define: Used to understand the exact meaning of a word, phrase, or concept. For example:

```
• Define the term 'neural network' in the
  context of artificial intelligence.
• Define what 'Blockchain technology'
  means.
• Define the concept of 'globalization'.
```

Describe: Helpful when seeking a detailed understanding of a concept, process, or event. For example,

```
• Describe the process of mitosis in cell
  division.
• Describe how a combustion engine works.
• Describe the life cycle of a butterfly.
```

Explain: Useful to understand the 'why' or 'how' of a concept. For example, "Explain how a bill becomes law."

- *Explain how the greenhouse effect contributes to global warming.*
- *Explain how artificial intelligence works.*
- *Explain why diversity is important in a workplace*

Clarify: Good for getting additional details or simplicity when a concept seems confusing. For example

- *Could you clarify what is meant by 'quantum computing'?*
- *Could you clarify the concept of 'the butterfly effect' in chaos theory?*
- *Could you clarify what 'dark matter' refers to in astronomy?*

Exemplify: A request for examples to illustrate a concept or idea. For example, "Can you exemplify the concept of 'natural selection' with real-world instances?"

- *Can you exemplify 'classical conditioning' using everyday situations?*
- *Can you exemplify the concept of 'economies of scale' with real-world examples?*
- *Can you exemplify 'cognitive dissonance' with practical instances*

Compare and Contrast: Helpful to understand similarities and differences between two or more concepts. For example, "Compare and contrast photosynthesis and cellular respiration."

- *Compare and contrast capitalism and socialism.*

- *Compare and contrast classical and operant conditioning.*
- *Compare and contrast renewable and nonrenewable energy sources.*

Summarize: Useful for condensing large amounts of information into a succinct form. For example

- *Summarize the main theories of personality psychology.*
- *Summarize the causes and effects of the Great Depression.*
- *Summarize the contributions of Albert Einstein to the field of physics.*

Analyze: A deeper level of understanding, where you break down a complex concept into its components. For example

- *Analyze the effects of deforestation on global biodiversity.*
- *Analyze the impact of the internet on communication.*
- *Analyze the role of the protagonist in the novel "To Kill a Mockingbird".*

Evaluate or Critique: Involves forming judgments about the value or quality of something. For example

- *Evaluate the pros and cons of nuclear energy.*
- *Critique the portrayal of society in George Orwell's "1984".*
- *Evaluate the implications of artificial intelligence for job security.*

Predict: Useful for using existing knowledge to make educated guesses about future events. For example, "Predict the impact of climate change on polar ice caps."

- *Predict the impact of advancements in technology on education.*
- *Predict the future of space exploration given current technological trends.*
- *Predict the consequences of continuous deforestation for the Earth's climate.*

Apply or Implement: Useful for understanding how to use a concept in a practical context. For example,

- *How could we implement renewable energy solutions in a small town?*
- *How can I apply the concept of mindfulness to reduce stress?*
- *How can I apply Minimalism?*

These words are commonly used in learning environments to encourage critical thinking, understanding, and effective communication and act as guideposts for deep, engaging and meaningful conversations

Think of these terms as navigational aids on the sea of knowledge. They are tools you can use to dig deeper into any subject, they help with confusion, and understanding. Use them wisely, and you will find that it makes learning actually and when you have having fun and understanding concents at the same time it is great feeling. In the upcoming section , we're going to dive into the best practices for learning.

Best Practices for Using ChatGPT for Learning:

By asking well-researched and detailed questions, you can unlock a wealth of knowledge on a particular subject or topic. You can use it in whatever walk of life whether you're a student studying for exams, an entrepreneur seeking to broaden your business acumen, or a professional looking to elevate your career, the pursuit of learning is an ongoing journey of discovery and growth. Learning is a lifelong process that isn't restricted by age, profession, or status.

I am going to provide you with multiple ways and examples where you can use ChatGPT to learn anything you want.

Apply this advice that you are getting here with your desired subjects:

Ask ChatGPT to explain a particular concept from multiple perspectives:

```
"Could you please explain the concept of recycling from an environmental, economic, and social perspective?"
```

Make it help you understand a difficult topic in greater depth:

```
"I'm having trouble understanding how photosynthesis works. Could you break it down and explain it in a more simple way?"
```

Ask ChatGPT to provide you with advice or strategies to help you gain a better understanding of a particular concept:

```
"I'm finding it hard to grasp the principles of algebra. What strategies or methods can I use to understand it better?"
```

Make it discuss a particular concept from its various interpretations:

```
"Could you discuss the concept of 'happiness' from various psychological perspectives such as cognitive, behavioral, and humanistic psychology?"
```

Ask specific questions about information you need:

"Please provide me the annual budget Nasa had from 1970 to 2020"

Have it breakdown a particular topic or problem into its various components:

"Chan you help me break down the concept of healthy eating into its various components like nutritional balance, portion control, and meal timing?"

You can request ChatGPT to explain different concepts in personalized ways in order to gain a comprehensive understanding. Additionally, you can ask follow-up questions to gain further clarity and to gain a more detailed understanding.

Request to create a learning plan.

You can also use ChatGPT to create lesson plans. You can provide it with a detailed explanation of what you would like to learn, and the system will generate insights into how you can create an effective plan to meet your goals. Additionally, ChatGPT can offer advice on how to break down the material into smaller components in order to make the learning process more efficient and effective.

Example: "Help me create a learning plan to learn about [topic]. I need advice on how to structure my plan, what topics to focus on, and what resources I should use. I would like this plan to cover the material in one month".

When you provide an explanation of your goals, it will come with tips and strategies on how to create and customize a learning plan that is tailored to your needs and timeline.

ChatGPT can generate an outline of topics to study, suggest resources, and provide quizzes for reinforcement, Before asking ChatGPT for a learning plan, clearly define what you want to learn or achieve. This should include key topics to cover, subtopics, and a possible sequence to follow.

Learning Difficult Concepts with ChatGPT

Learning difficult concepts with ChatGPT can be easier if you know how to use it effectively.

- **Start with a general understanding:** If a concept is completely new, ask ChatGPT to explain it in simple terms or like you're a five-year-old. It can help lay a foundation for more complex explanations.

Example Prompt: `"Explain quantum physics like I'm five."`

- **Break down the concept:** If the concept is too complicated, break it down. Ask ChatGPT to explain individual components of the concept one at a time.

Example Prompt: `"Explain the concept of superposition in quantum physics."`

Ask ChatGPT to explain each concept in multiple ways in order to gain a better understanding of the material. If you don't understand it in a certain way ask it to explain it in a different way.. Understanding complex subjects often requires breaking down the topic into smaller, digestible components and dissect the subject matter, allowing learners to build their understanding block by block.

For instance, if you're studying climate change, you could ask, `"Can you break down the topic of climate change into smaller components for me?"` In response, ChatGPT might suggest components such as 'Understanding the Greenhouse Effect', 'Causes of Climate Change', 'Impacts of Climate Change', 'Climate Change Mitigation Strategies', and 'Controversies and Debates about Climate Change'.

Each of these components could be studied individually, allowing for a more targeted and efficient learning process.

- Ask to provide examples and additional resources to help with comprehension of the subject.

ChatGPT can be utilized not only for direct explanations but also for providing valuable examples and resources to enhance the comprehension of a subject.

Let's use the stock market as an example, ChatGPT can break it down and provide examples or resources that simplify the subject. For example:

"Could you explain the concept of a stock split with an example?"

With a query like this it will provide a simplified explanation, Like comparing a stock split to slicing a pizza. You still have the same amount of pizza (or company ownership), but it's divided into more smaller slices (or shares). This makes each slice more affordable, even though the total value of the pizza remains the same.

Furthermore, to supplement your understanding, you could ask for additional resources:

"Can you recommend books, articles, or online courses that explain the basics of the stock market for beginners?"

In response, ChatGPT could suggest reputable financial education websites, influential investment books, or even online courses available on platforms like Coursera or Khan Academy.

Step by step learning:

Step-by-step learning process can illuminate how each part connects to the larger picture.

Prompt examples for step-by-step learning:

- "Can you explain the steps to get started with real state?"
- "What are the steps involved in learning how to code in Python?"
- "Can you describe the process of learning a new language, such as Spanish?"
- "Guide me through the stages of understanding the human circulatory system for my biology class."
- "What are the steps to becoming proficient in graphic design?"
- "What are the steps to understanding the basic principles of economics?"
- "Can you guide me through the steps of learning how to cook Italian cuisine?"
- "Provide a step-by-step plan for learning the basics of digital marketing."

Remember to use these prompts as starting points and refine them based on your specific learning goals and personal understanding of the subject matter. By providing ChatGPT with an explanation of the learning goal and material to be studied, it can provide detailed explanations, advice, and resources to help the user reach their learning goals.

Explaining "As If":

Explaining something "As If" can be used to gain comprehension about something you don't understand to something you do understand. In this way you can gain an understanding of a subject from a perspective that is familiar to you. This can be especially effective when struggling to understand a complex concept.

- Can you explain the concept of cryptocurrencies **as if** I'm a 10-year-old?"
- Can you explain how airplanes fly **as if** I have no background in physics?
- Can you explain the importance of the tea ceremony in Japanese culture **as if** I'm someone who has never been exposed to Asian cultures before?"
- Can you explain the principles of quantum physics **as if** it were a detective story?"

In all of those examples, the goal is to break down complex subjects in a way that is more manageable for you to understand. This method simplifies your learning and adds an element of relatability, making learning not only more effective but also more enjoyable for you.

Gaining Clarification:

Using ChatGPT for gaining clarification can be a great way to solidify your understanding of a concept. Clarification helps to ensure that you have a complete and accurate understanding of a subject before attempting to apply, explain, or analyze it. You are not always going to understand something the first time is being explained to you. When you find yourself in that situation requesting the AI clarification helps identify any gaps in your knowledge as well as misunderstanding you may have about the subject. You may need some additional information for the subject to make sense to you, and that is completely normal. You will need to use this method a lot when you are learning complex subjects that are not easy to understand.

Here are examples of prompts that range from simple to more complex subjects:

Simple Subject - Cooking:

```
"Could you clarify what 'al dente' means in
cooking pasta?"
```

Intermediate Subject - Basic Astronomy:

```
"I'm confused about the difference between a
solar and lunar eclipse. Could you clarify
that for me?"
```

More Complex Subject - Basic Computer Programming:

```
"I'm having difficulty understanding the
concept of object-oriented programming. Could
you help clarify it?"
```

Advanced Subject - Economics:

```
"ChatGPT, can you clarify the concept of
'opportunity cost' in economics?"
```

Complex Subject - Quantum Physics:

```
"ChatGPT, could you clarify what 'quantum
entanglement' means? I'm finding it a tough
concept to grasp."
```

Remember that the complexity of the topic doesn't limit the usefulness of ChatGPT. The AI model can help clarify concepts across a wide range of subjects, from simple everyday tasks to complex academic theories. So the process is basically to follow your own pace and gain comprehension little by little about the subject.

Hack #6 Teach it to write like you and create content in your own style

By giving ChatGPT existing samples of your writing, you can educate it to write in your own distinctive manner. It is very simple you have to provide pure examples of your writing and ask the AI to write a piece of writing in that style. The more examples you provide, the better the system will learn how you write as you, and as the AI continues to give you examples of your style, it will continue learning from the input and feedback you can give it.

In order to start teaching ChatGPT your writing style you have to provide it with examples of your own writing. The longer, the better. The AI will learn things like your sentence structure, vocabulary, and tone, along with other details of the style of your writing.

Example:

"I am going to provide you with a piece of my own writing. After reading this, please write a paragraph on [topic] imitating my style. Understand?"

"Next, I will share an example of my writing style, After you've processed this, I'd like you to generate a [content] that mirrors this style."

"Please take note of my writing style in the upcoming text. Once you've understood it, I would like you to mimic this style by …."

After a prompt like that ChatGPT will tell you that it understands and then you can provide the text, and ChatGPT will originate the text in that style. ChatGPT will not accurately capture your style correctly the first time, you have to keep providing examples and asking to review and retry to perfect the output.

Keep The conversations saved and come back to it:

Save the conversation and when you want to write in your own style, go back to that saved conversation so you don't have to teach it all over again

Multiple Attempts: The thing about this is that it will take multiple attempts to get the desired output.

Do The Final Touches Yourself: No matter how hard and how many times you try, ChatGPT is not going to capture all the nuances of your individual style perfectly. It will save you time to write everything yourself but the finishing touches are yours to make. Take the time to go over it yourself and refine it with your own edits and additions.

So keep the following bullet points in mind:

- You can teach ChatGPT to write in your own distinctive style by providing it with examples of your writing.
- Longer examples of your writing style are preferred, but shorter samples can also be useful for teaching it.
- To improve ChatGPT's ability to mimic your writing style, you should offer feedback and input as it continues to learn and generate content.

- Create a diverse and extensive dataset of your own writing to capture the nuances of your style, including sentence structures, vocabulary, tone, and different types of writing.
- Giving specific writing samples or instructions can help ensure the desired results.
- If the generated text doesn't match your expectations, you can use example pieces, explicit stylistic instructions, keywords, saved conversations, and multiple attempts, and make the final touches yourself to refine the output.

Hack #7 Summarize

ChatGPT has the ability to understand the context and content given. And with this ability, it can generate concise summaries in a fraction of the time that it would take you for doing it manually. This makes it an invaluable tool for those who need to quickly and accurately consensus lengthy documents into shorter digestible summaries.

Examples of summary prompts:

"I am going to provide you with a piece of text. Could you summarize the main points for me?"

"Could you please read the following text and provide a concise summary of its main ideas?"

"I'm having trouble understanding this material. Could you distill it into a few key points?"

"I'm looking to grasp the essence of this document. Can you summarize its main concepts in simpler terms?"

"I've got this long piece of text here. Can you condense its main themes into a brief summary?"

You can even mix this up with the browsing beta feature we showed you earlier. (To summarize website content) You can provide links to ChatGPT and ask it to summarize the content of that specific website. As we mentioned before, make sure it is a website that you can access with the link alone and that there are no login requirements.

Example: `"Can you summarize this article for me?"` (and provide a URL or paste the article text)

Provide clear instructions if you want to summarize a specific section, for example, `"Can you summarize the main points of the following paragraph?"` or `"Please provide a brief summary of the section on [topic]."` You can also indicate the desired length that you want for your summary.

It is very easy and straightforward. You can provide the prompt first, and they say, "Understand?" and then provide the text later once ChatGPT confirms or just do it at the same prompt—both work.

AI, The Future of work and the Next Chapter of Human Progress

This world is changing fast. By the end of the decade (2030) AI will already revolutionize the way we live and work. It will have a massive impact on many industries, with the potential to automate many different processes, reduce costs, improve efficiencies, and create new products and services. But it will also come with side effects that are hard to predict just yet.

AI is a rapidly growing multi-billion dollar industry, and according to a tudy done by Brookings, artificial intelligence technologies could increase global GDP by $15.7 trillion.

Breakdown of GDP increases **by region:**

- $7 trillion in China
- $3.7 trillion in North America

- $1.8 trillion in Northern Europe
- $1.2 trillion for Africa and Oceania
- $0.9 trillion in the rest of Asia outside of China
- $0.7 trillion in Southern Europe
- $0.5 trillion in Latin America

Artificial intelligence has been described as a fourth industrial revolution. The effects of AI in our world are going to be profound and pervasive. Not only it will change entire industries and economies, but it will also have significant ramifications for governments and societal structures around the world.

So AI will cause massive disruptions in the workforce over the next few years. It is going to touch all sectors and industries, it is clear at this point that some industries will expand, others will evolve, and entirely new ones will be created, but others may disappear entirely. So the rise of AI isn't without its casualties.

Certain industries, especially those heavily reliant on routine, manual labor, face the risk of becoming obsolete. For instance, with the advent of autonomous vehicles, traditional roles in the transportation sector, like trucking or taxi services, might face significant disruption in the way that they will need less and less human labor as time goes on. The same holds for manufacturing jobs, where automation is already replacing human labor in many areas.

There is going to be job displacement but also job creation. The 2030s will be very different from than 2020s. Jobs in AI development, data science, robotics, and related areas are expected to grow while tasks that require more human-automated workers like manufacturing and logistics, are expected to be reduced more in more as AI keeps advancing, forcing workers in many industries to adapt and acquire new skill sets related to these emerging technologies.

Upskilling and lifelong learning will start becoming a necessity for both individuals and businesses. The workplace of the future will require quick adaptation from people, jobs that require knowledge, information, and cognitive skills will be needed a lot more than physical labor. You will need it to remain relevant and successful in this fast-changing environment.

Considering human nature to have governing system in place where a few benefit while the masses are excluded. It is possible that the benefits of AI will not be uniformly distributed, meaning that it can cause economic disparities both within and between countries. Just as wealth and power are currently concentrated in the hands of a few, the benefits of AI are disproportionately received by those in a position of advantage. This is often due to factors such as education, wealth, and access to technology but also by individuals who take action and those who don't.

For example, the automation of jobs poses a significant threat to low-skilled workers who are more likely to be replaced by AI than those with high-skill ocupations. These type of scenarios will likely lead to unemployment and economic inequality. It is true that a lot of jobs will be created with AI, but those jobs are likely to require skills that many displaced workers do not possess.

Secondly, the concentration of AI expertise and infrastructure in developed countries could exacerbate global inequalities. Because some countries will have a head start in harnessing the power of AI will others will not start until later. So if that's the case some countries will enjoy the benefits of AI earlier than others. If we do not expect this problem and let it happen, we could be in a situation where s small number of countries dominate the global economy leading to even more wealth inequality since we already have countries with more wealth, influence, and power than others.

These are just some of the risks out there related to AI. Governments around the world should be aware of the many challenges we are going to face as a society, and we should prioritize lifelong learning no ensure people with low resources can adapt to the changing job market. Governments may need to look at the idea of Welfare systems such UBI unemployment gets out of control for those jobs that have been lost and replaced by automation.

Here's a broad categorization of how industries might be evolved, created, or displaced due to AI:

Industries that Will Evolve:

- Healthcare: AI could revolutionize diagnostics, patient care, personalized medicine, and hospital management.
- Education: AI-powered personalized learning, online learning platforms, and administrative automation are expected to reshape education.
- Retail: From customer service chatbots to predictive inventory management, AI is transforming the retail industry.
- Finance: AI is set to change banking and insurance with automated financial advice, fraud detection, risk assessment, and algorithmic trading.
- Transportation and Logistics: Autonomous vehicles, intelligent routing, predictive maintenance, and AI-powered supply chain optimization will transform this industry.
- Agriculture: Precision agriculture, enabled by AI and machine learning, can lead to more efficient farming practices.
- Manufacturing: AI, combined with robotics, can optimize production lines, improve quality control, and create smarter supply chains.

New Industries that Might be Created:

- AI Ethics: With AI becoming ubiquitous, there will be a growing need for specialists in AI ethics to ensure the responsible use of the technology.

- Data Privacy and Security: With increasing reliance on AI and data, there will be an increased demand for data privacy and security services.
- Robotics and Automation Solutions: As businesses across industries adopt AI, there will be a growing market for companies that can provide tailored automation solutions.

Industries Likely to be Displaced or Transformed:

- Manufacturing: As mentioned, AI and automation will likely displace many traditional manufacturing jobs.
- Customer Service: AI-powered chatbots and virtual assistants are likely to replace many customer service roles.
- Data Entry: AI and automation are likely to displace jobs that involve repetitive, predictable tasks like data entry.
- Transportation: The rise of autonomous vehicles could disrupt the need for human drivers in trucking, taxis, and delivery services.

AI has its potential but it also has its risks, in the near future when most of the writing content, images, and videos will be AI-generated it is expected that we could have a problem with deepfakes (fabricated audiovisual representations created with sophisticated AI techniques) These synthetic portrayals are so convincing that they can trick people into believing things are real when they are not—blurring the line between fact and fiction and raising fundamental questions about truth in the digital age. This rising threat can manipulate or completely fabricate digital content with amazing accuracy. If governments don't find a way to prevent, regulate and punish this, it will lead to the spread of disinformation and fraud as well as public mistrust on everything we see online and even unrest. This is already an ongoing problem where deepfakes have already been used to deceive companies into transferring money. Governments will need to make sure they are aware and treat these issues accordingly.

AI algorithms will become increasingly sophisticated, in fact, 10x more powerful than they are now just like every new technology that was first created. AI has already begun to reshape our perception of reality in subtle yet significant ways. This metamorphosis is largely attributable to the personalization algorithms powering our digital lives and the echo chambers they create, affecting our access to information and influencing our worldview. We need to make sure this transformative and dangerous potential of AI does not make significant impacts on our perception of reality. There is only so much individuals can prepare on their own, and typically then can only help themselves. We need world governments to take action, dive into these risks and introduce legislation and regulation so AI doesn't get out of hand. Also, As AI becomes more integrated into society, there's a growing need for the public to understand how it works and its potential impact so it is used for the good. So we are going to need proper updates in our education systems. There is a lot of work ahead to ensure AI doesn't exacerbate social inequalities, make AI systems more transparent, fair, and secure. Also, nations need to work together on transferring information, and bilateral agreements, among other things, since AI doesn't know borders.

We also need to be careful with the bias these systems have been trained on, creators of AI technologies will place algorithms that can inadvertently perpetuate and even amplify these biases, leading to outcomes where it favors a particular issue over another and has no consideration about common sense. Remember that AI doesn't possess the human capability to question the fairness or correctness of the data they have been trained on (yet), so they simply just mimic patterns of data it has been trained on, sometimes pushing agendas or maintaining certain power structures.

So AI will undoubtedly bring significant benefits to society, and we covered them throughout the book, but there will also be many side effects such as unemployment, privacy concerns, misinformation, and dependency, among others.

To add up another one, there are concerns that AI is not being deployed and introduced to society in a responsible manner, there is a startling statistic where 50% of AI researchers believe there's a 10% or greater chance that humans could go extinct due to our inability to control AI. But we can only speculate now. We have to see how things will develop over the next few years, let's hope the world governments start taking action about all of this soon so we can ensure we can enjoy the benefits of AI and avoid a worst-case scenario.

In the meantime, it is up to you to learn everything you can about AI and take action every day and get these benefits to help yourself and those around you. The benefits that can be reaped from this not only serve to enhance your personal growth but also extend to those in your sphere of influence.

It is your responsibility to make things happen. Throughout the book, you've encountered various businesses already established where you can use AI to scale quickly. And even if you were not into it you were given instructions to learn to locate such opportunities that will fit your persona and personal circumstances. We wanted to provide an approach that suits your unique situation. Keep in mind that identifying the right opportunity for you can sometimes be a time-consuming process. It can probably take months. It is important to be patient and thorough in your research, it's equally vital to take action and immerse yourself in the field. The balance between patient discovery and being proactive action is key. Take a moment to reflect on your personal goals in the context of what you've learned. Consider how you can integrate AI into your own life and work, and set clear, actionable steps towards achieving these goals.

If you found this book to be informative and helpful, please consider leaving a review. Your feedback not only aids us in improving future editions but also helps more people to make a decision if this will work for them.

Made in the USA
Monee, IL
25 September 2023

286a1d5a-43b3-49c7-8232-b6e0cd1db91fR01